THOMAS HORNSBY FERRIL
AND THE AMERICAN WEST

*Edited by Robert C. Baron, Stephen J. Leonard,
and Thomas J. Noel*

FULCRUM PUBLISHING
GOLDEN, COLORADO

*and the Center of the American West
University of Colorado at Boulder*

Copyright © 1996 Thomas Hornsby Ferril Literary Trust
and Fulcrum Publishing

Interior photographs and illustration (p. 150) courtesy of Anne Ferril Folsom
except where noted. Portrait of Thomas Hornsby Ferril on page 1, courtesy
of the Denver Public Library Western History Department.

Interior design and limited edition cover by Bill Spahr
Paperback cover design by Deborah Rich

Library of Congress Cataloging-in-Publication Data

Ferril, Thomas Hornsby, 1896–1988
  [Selections. 1996]
    Thomas Hornsby Ferril and the American West / edited by Robert C.
Baron, Stephen J. Leonard, and Thomas J. Noel.
      p.   cm.
    Includes a selection of Ferril's prose and poetry, along with critical
essays.
    Includes bibliographical references.
    ISBN 1-55591-334-2
    ISBN 1-55591-339-3 (lim. ed.)
  1. West (U.S.) — Literary collections. 2. Ferril, Thomas Hornsby, 1896–
1988 — Criticism and interpretation. 3. West (U.S.) — In literature. 4.
Nature in literature. I. Baron, Robert C. II. Leonard, Stephen J. III.
Noel, Thomas J. (Thomas Jacob) IV. Title.
PS3511.E7245A6 1996
811'.52 — dc20   96-28648
                                                                  CIP

Printed in the United States of America

0 9 8 7 6 5 4 3 2 1

Fulcrum Publishing
350 Indiana Street, Suite 350
Golden, Colorado 80401-5093
(800) 992-2908 • (303) 277-1623

TABLE OF CONTENTS

SELECTED POEMS

SELECTED PROSE

Publisher's Preface

Robert C. Baron

In his essay "Walking," Henry David Thoreau wrote, "Eastward I go only by force; but westward I go free." And John Muir once wrote that "The mountains are fountains of men as well as of rivers, of glaciers, of fertile soil. The great poets, philosophers, prophets, able men whose thoughts and deeds have moved the world, have come down from the mountains."

American intellectuals have always been ambivalent about the West, believing that the edge of culture, art, and the world of ideas lay slightly to the west of Concord, Massachusetts, just beyond Worcester and certainly no further west than the Allegheny Mountains. How could they deal with a major American poet who lived in Colorado and wrote about the mountains and the plains? Thomas Hornsby Ferril has been called a regional poet, assuming somehow that the Rocky Mountain West is a smaller canvas than the ponds and hills of Thoreau's and Emerson's Concord or the farms of Frost's Vermont. T.S. Eliot once said, "The great poet, in writing himself, writes his time," and Ferril was certainly no exception to this idea.

Thomas Hornsby Ferril was born in Denver on February 25, 1896. A number of events have been planned in honor of the centennial of Ferril's birth, and this book is a part of that celebration. We asked many of Ferril's friends which of his works they would like to see included in a centennial edition. The result is this collection of seventy-six of Ferril's best poems, five of his prose pieces, a personal essay from his daughter, Anne Ferril Folsom, and essays from fifteen other contributors.

I would like to thank all of those individuals who have taken pleasure in the creation of this book with their contributions, stories, and writings. Special thanks to Dr. John Buechner, Patty Limerick, and Bill Hornby and to my coeditors Tom Noel and Steve Leonard. I would like to thank Daniel Forrest-Bank and Bill Spahr for their editorial and design work. I also wish to thank the Literary Estate of Thomas Hornsby Ferril, Yale University Press, Harper Brothers, William Morrow, Ahsahta Press, *The Rocky Mountain Herald*, the *Rocky Mountain News*, and others who have allowed us to reprint the works of Ferril.

This has been an exciting and happy project to work on—a project measured not only by the quality of Ferril's writing but also by the life of this special man. Many have shared in the joy of Thomas Hornsby Ferril's life and have felt his impact on both his many friends and the community in which he worked, wrote, and participated. We hope you enjoy reading this book and learning more about the life and work of this important national poet.

Memory and Motion:
Almost Holding Our Own

Patricia Nelson Limerick

>⊷⊶⊙⊷⊷⊰

The lady is sleeping longer
in her chair.

Sometimes she touches
her long long hair
as if the girl
who wore the hair
were there.

Nineteen hundred and ninety-six is the centennial of Thomas Hornsby Ferril's birth. For the American West, the last century has been a roller coaster ride through history. Events have rushed by at an unforgiving and disorienting pace; hundreds of thousands of people have moved into the region. The years between 1886 and 1996 have indeed been, to use one of Ferril's phrases, a "trial by time." Given the opportunity at contemplation afforded by his centennial, "How might we best," as Ferril himself put it, "Unwind a hundred years?"

The answer is an easy one. To keep from unwinding ourselves, we need what Ferril offers us: a counterforce to the loss of moorings and bearings in a society driven by mobility. We need an antidote to an historically induced condition of "motion sickness" that has particularly afflicted the Western United States. And memory, that property of the human mind that robs time of its power to erase and disorient, is surely that antidote.

Thomas Hornsby Ferril was one of the most skilled and graceful of practitioners when it came to the prescription and application of memory's powers. To Ferril, memory was a substance as actual as earth and water. When he walked along a mountain stream or down a Denver street, he saw the past—both geological and historical—nearly as clearly and vividly as he saw the present.

Ferril *heard* the past as well as saw it, his was a mind in frequent conversation with the women and men of Colorado, dead and alive. When Ferril's "hunger for what has been" gripped him, he summoned the past into his company and then quizzed it with good-natured but pointed questions. Manifesting itself in ghost towns as well as individual ghosts, buildings long abandoned as well as trails, streets, and roads heavily layered with history, the past talked back, and Ferril wrote down its responses. "The snows," as he wrote, "have melted questions into answers."

Two rivers converged long before the city of Denver occurred, and Ferril wrote of the people who met and built the city on the site where those rivers came together: "They told me while I stared down at the water:/*If you will stay we will not go away.*" Ferril stayed, and the people of Colorado's past stayed with him.

Ferril, moreover, fully recognized that his immediate experience would itself evolve into memory, and that his very vigorous presence would, in time, become an absence. "The time it takes for not yet being dead/Is ticking in the watches" of the people around him, he knew. "Today," Ferril said, "is going to be long long ago," He knew that graves and ruins, the places where the dead quite literally held their ground, record the *vitality* of those who once lived, as well as their mortality. Thus, in his mind, melancholy was only one of many emotions evoked by the presence of the dead; empathy and exuberance were equally important.

At the other end of the life span, children figure frequently in Ferril's poems, as representations of the future and as reminders that even those who have arrived at the status of "elderly" launched their journey from the port of infancy, a fact spotlit by the observance of Ferril's own birth. In "The Prairie Melts," a child of the distant future—"A child far-generated, lover to lover,/Lover to lover, lover to lover over ... ,"—walks the land where Ferril once stood and, despite distance in time, still finds the land familiar. "They told me of this prairie," the child says: "This is the prairie where they used to come/To watch the lilies and to watch the falcons." In "Cadetta—C & S," children, vigorously quizzing their elders about what lies ahead, ride a train into the mountains; in the baggage car ahead of them rides a corpse. This is not a horror story, Ferril's reflective tone tells his readers; this is just one version of the journey we take in the course of every day, with life and death as our fellow passengers.

An observer with such an alert recognition of the passage of time had every reason to contemplate the ambitions of the twentieth century with wonder, as well as with a raised eyebrow. Ferril drew an entirely recognizable portrait of an architect who "got a job promoting the newest highest building higher than the newest highest building with the newest highest ear-pop elevators musiking up ... ." This look, through Ferril's eyes, at the way in which a mounting cycle of ambition was ratcheting up the Denver skyline, lets loose the recognition that today's high-rises are going to make for some remarkable ruins. The archaeologists of the future, those who would "sift" the "shards and middens" of this city, had better come prepared to deal in bulk.

In cities and in mountains, time and its passage provided Ferril with his terrain of adventure. He saw mountains as matter in motion; the sediment load carried by a river was a mountain melting. A particular, vivid glimpse of birds in flight, a moment of sharpened awareness in the present, provided its own occasion for an extended look down the corridors of time:

The hawks are circling the western cliffs
Over the bones of hawks
That circled the western cliffs
Over the bones of hawks.

When Ferril gazed, unblinking, at the workings of time, motion and stability ceased to be opposites and experimented with collaboration.

Birds in flight, wagons crossing plains, rivers wearing down mountains, walkers on the shores of city lakes, horseback riders on mountain trails, cars on roads: Ferril's poems are full of forces, creatures, and people in motion. With his attention captured by a flock of birds fighting against a stiff plain's wind, Ferril forged an unforgettable image of motion and stability in alliance: he looked up and saw, he said, "a treadmill of swallows almost holding their own."

In every Ferril poem, human consciousness beats against the powerful force of time and almost holds its own. "What keeps on moving if your body stops?" Ferril asked. In his case, we know the answer.

Ferril died in 1988. His poems keep moving.

Ferril and the West

Dr. John C. Buechner

>─┤◆⟩─○─⟨◆┤─<

In my years at Colorado's Capitol building, both as a member of the legislature and as an educator working with its many committees, I have been struck by the pride my colleagues take in the words of Tom Ferril, paired with the murals of Allen True in the huge rotunda dome. Many times I have seen legislators, citizens of Colorado, and visitors look up at those poetic words and paintings. All of them seem a little prouder of Colorado for the experience, especially when they go up to the top of the Capitol or on its west porch to look out toward the Rockies across the urban scene. With Ferril's words and an extraordinary landscape meeting in their minds, they begin to understand the Rocky Mountain West.

Here are Ferril's words from under the Capitol dome:

Here is a land where life is written in water,
The West is where the water was and is,

Father and son of old, mother and daughter,
Following rivers up immensities
Of range and desert, thirsting the sundown ever,
Crossing a hill to climb a hill still drier,
Naming tonight a city by some river
A different name from last night's camping fire.

Look to the green within the mountain cup,
Look to the prairie parched for water lack,
Look to the sun that pulls the oceans up,
Look to the cloud that gives the oceans back,
Look to your heart and may your wisdom grow
To power of lightning and to peace of snow.

The good wisdom of the legislature in using Ferril's words as a force for education within the Capitol reminds us of the role the humanities play in guiding the spirit by which we make our homes in this place called Colorado. Despite the many differences that might divide us in our daily lives, our Colorado poets, our novelists, and our essayists steadily remind us of the common loyalties and deeper meanings of life that link us as human beings committed to living in this particular place.

The Center of the American West at the University of Colorado is proud to have had a role in bringing Thomas Hornsby Ferril's work back to public attention in this centennial volume. In the 1990s, it is the University's goal to reach outward from the campus and take part in an extended conversation with the people of the state, and the activities of the Center of the American West form a central part of that campaign. Unless higher education marshals the best of a state's and a region's culture and shares it with the citizens, it will not have done its job in holding our distinctive regional civilization together in these difficult times of change and controversy.

A fine poet such as Tom Ferril is perhaps the best guide on the trail toward pride in Colorado as a place, and toward pride in our people in all their diversity. Pride in ourselves is the essential foundation for building the better future we all want. Education is vital, and Tom Ferril, in addition to his many other roles so well described in this book, was an educator—"Look to your heart and may your wisdom grow/To power of lightning and to peace of snow." Ferril, among Colorado's many fine writers, was the most persistent in asking his fellow citizens to search their hearts for wisdom, and in believing that the search would be successful.

Selected Poems

Thomas Hornsby Ferril

Always Begin Where You Are

Always begin right here where you are
And work out from here:
If adrift, feel the feel of the oar in the oarlock first,
If saddling a horse let your right knee slug
The belly of the horse like an uppercut,
Then cinch his suck,
Then mount and ride away
To any dream deserving the sensible world.

Barbed Wire Gates

The gates I open cannot swing,
They are barbed wire and no one knows,
Who sees me lift and fasten them,
How hard they are to close.

For every gate I have let down
I must close two, now you have passed,
A gate for you, a gate for me,
With barbed wire twisted fast.

I will be closing gates for you
So far away you cannot tell
If I am there at all or if
The gates are fastened well.

American Testament

Where were their myths, if these were beautiful?
Was Daphne there, beloved of Apollo?

Kentucky was too dark and red with blood,
But Amos cut a path that Ruth could follow.

If these were bold in dreams, what Centaur's child
As fair as Jason ever led them on?

Job, in his bull-boat on the brown Missouri,
Slept while Ezekiel pushed a pole till dawn.

Calypso where? Was Niobe among them
With sorrow singing in her sons and daughters?

Isaiah, wounded by the Arkansas,
Heard Ezra's oxen drowning in the waters.

How were they beautiful without Diana?
Was there a valley of unwaking youth?

Jude took a squaw out of the Taos moonlight,
Joel bought a lover with a grizzly tooth.

If there was courage in their brutal being,
Was it not ugly gods that drove them on?

At eighty Daniel whistled hymns in Juarez,
And snow-white Joshua reached Oregon.

Answers

The poets sing of I so much,
Who is this I?
Whoever sees, as through their souls, the world,
And hears the sky.

To you the poets write so much,
And who are you?
Whoever listens at the gates of night
For what rings through.

Of beauty poets tell so much,
Why speak they so?
Because they know it is, yet where nor why,
They never know.

Blind words the poets use so much,
Why are they blind?
Such fetters they must wear to grope for what
They cannot find.

If poets wander in the dark,
Why must they speak?
To fight the lamp for men too strong to know
That men are weak.

How do the poets know so well
That they are right?
They never know, yet ever feel the truth
In second sight.

Then who will prove that what is sung
Be more than breath?
None but such dead as none can prove
Had smiled at death.

Basket

The children out of the shade have brought me a basket
Very small and woven of dry grass
Smelling as sweet in December as the day
I smelled it first.
                    Only one other ever
Was this to me, sweet birch from a far river,
You would not know, you did not smell the birch,
You would not know, you did not smell the grass,
You did not know me then.

Blossom Rock

Gold was the blossom of the evening primrose,
Gold was the blossom of the buffalo bur,
Gold was the blossom of the golden buckwheat,
Gold was your golden hair.

Beyond What Ranges?

Tell me, beyond what ranges of the reasonable will
Does faring of a city quest?

I ask you this in Denver, Colorado,
Lip of the bulldozer against the skull,
Churning the dead to furrows of new exile,
Numb as the pistons when the diesels cool
And the steel crane nods
A dragline sag
Down the sandpit pools of evening.

They say a child was drowned today in a sandpit.

I near remember how it used to be
The very morning of this very day:
These pools of sandpit water were not here;
Instead there towered a high and yellow bluff
Yucca-dry as the spiney blink of a horned-toad;
The bluff sheered back ten cottonwood shadows from
The bake of the raw-hide shrink of the river bed;
Gophers, cactus, chattering cater-cousin,
Strawberry runners of the buffalo grass
Clamping the powdered herd songs of far cattle,
Every root in place and nothing trembling
But a whisp of dusty whirlwind spiraling off
Like a girl-child losing a tune she nearly danced to.
How came these waters deep so suddenly?
How was the great bluff moiled, unsocketed
And cast against the skyline of the sky,
Oracular mortar webbed of steel and dripping
To stiffen on the trestles of the westwind
Over the lintels of lightning?

They say a child was drowned today in a sandpit.
Who was the child?
Where did her people come from?

Blue-Stemmed Grass

There's blue-stemmed grass as far as I can see,
But when I take the blue-stemmed grass in hand,
And pull the grass apart, and speak the word
For every part, I do not understand
More than I understood of grass before.
"This part," I say, "is the straight untwisted awn,"
And "Here's the fourth glume of the sessile spikelet,"
And then I laugh out loud at what I've done.

I speak with reason to the blue-stemmed grass:
"This grass moves up through meadow beasts to men."
I weigh mechanical economies
Of meadow into flesh and back again.
I let the morning sun shine through my hand,
I trace the substance bloom and beast have given,
But I ask if phosphorus or nitrogen
Can make air through my lips mean hell or heaven.

All that the grass can make for any beast
Is here within my luminous hand of bone
And flesh and blood against the morning sun;
But I must listen alone, and you, alone,
Far children to be woven from green looms;
We move forever across meadows blowing,
But like no beast, we choke and cannot cry
When the grasses come, and when the grass is going.

Bookmarks

A bookmark for an album such as this,
Should be a ribbon with a cross-stitched phrase,
Pressed neatly into Milton's hymns of praise,
Yet here is none, but in this book of his,
That crossed the prairies with him long ago,
I find pale blades of buffalo grass to tell
Sweet pages where he could love Philomel,
And Phyllida and Cynthia and Chloe.
Here is a wedding song, stained by a leaf
Of mountain aspen, plucked when June was ripe;
If he marked other verse, I find no more,
But on one page, attuned to death and grief,
Are ashes from the embers of his pipe,
That must have spilled and did not reach the floor.

Bride

After the turgid incidence and when
The last mad whispering had darkly blown
Away, letting the woods be real again,
He propped his elbow on a lichened stone.
"I've climbed that mountain many times alone,"
He said at length. She stared, then asked him how
One felt at timberline. He answered "One
Feels much as we do now," remembering snow
That must have cooled whatever long ago
Had cracked the rocks with terrible ecstasy.
"It's not so wild up there, you feel as though
Something were finished. You're at peace with sky
And earth, as we are now." She pointed where
The peak seemed highest, whispering "Take me there."

Cadetta-C&S

They blow the whistle and they ring the bell,
The cross-ties on the railroad in the canyon
Cadetta
      cadetta
            cadetta
                  cadetta
                        cadetta
Like a stick on a picket fence
A dead boy harped.

Understand there's a corpse up ahead in the baggage car,
They told the brakeman not to build a fire,
Don't tell the children.

They say he was a mountain man who went
Down to the city and died and is going back.
Don't tell the children.

The children have never ridden the train before,
The children dream the train into the mountains,
Chug of the smokestack blacking aspen catkins,
They lean way out, they see the engineer
Chasing the mountains off the track like deer,
They taste the mountains tumbling through the windows,
They smell the lightning singed by rainy roses,
The river digs a tunnel under the train,
Now it is gone,
Now it is back again.

The train goes creaking through the air,
No wheels, no track, no flick of a lid to spare
From the terrible terrible big black rocks
And the waters chunking whiter than thunder
Over the train and under.

The pick, the axe, the shovel are painted red
In the glass box on the wall two cars ahead;
Where do they go? Why does the aisle of the car
Never come twisting back to where you are?

The corpse in the baggage car is three days new
And cool as the calico sunlight slanting through
The north-slope kinnikinnik the children stroke
With bells and eyelashes and engine smoke.

Few trendings of the world are in the corpse,
The drive wheels slip uphill, the canyon jerks
The pallid elements—lip, socket, bone,
Sagging uphill alone and home alone,
No pieces of ghost to hover or put together
But weight and tariff known to the brakeman's glove,
One box inside another,
No embers in the stove.

Bequeathed: no song of snows the forest caught,
No quit-claimed valleys time-locked in the vault,
No herds portfolio, no envelope
Of sweet grass greening up the aspen slope;
Bequeathed: no testament, no wax, no seal,
No lips to kiss, no fingertips to feel,
No files of ciphering accordion-pleated,
No ravenous heirs, no barrister mistreated,
Only a coming back from going down
To where each of the people was alone.

Now frolic, wild, and O how contrary,
The little train breaks through the canyon wall!
The mountains march away.
                              A valley spreads
Its grasses far and blue and over the heads
Of the children blows such pleasant earthlessness
They drowse and do not dream and float away

Beyond the yellow flowers and purple hay.

The engine stops.
                    The eyes, the ears of the children
Float back into their bodies sitting still
But moving, moving, why is stopping moving?
Why is the pine tree sliding up the hill?

The children lean across their windowsills,
The fireman pulls the cord that tolls the bell,
The baggageman and brakeman open the door,
They lift a wooden box to the mountain floor.

The train moves on,
The box is smaller and smaller
And smaller
            and smaller
                        and smaller
                                    and smaller
                                                and gone ...

Cadetta
        cadetta
                cadetta
                        cadetta
                                cadetta ...

Can I Bring Home?

Can I bring home the actual spider-spun
Geometry to prove what silk-to-spruce
And silk-to-alder over my brook have woven?
Or hearing the vesper sparrow, can I use
Again the very cry and the very hues
Of day dissolving in his dark wet throat?
How can I hold the antelope I lose
So instantly above the yucca butte?
What seizures drive so hard? What inventory
Of our acquisitive thrift or studied plunder?
Yet what deep love runs deeper in our story?
Do we not say forever: Share my wonder?
Do we not say: Behold what I have seen
That we may love for loving where we've been?

City Slipping Backward Into Tomorrow

What ever became of the boy
Struck down by a one-lung Cadillac
When he trotted into the street
To circle away from the house
With SCARLET FEVER on the door?

Caterpillars dripping from box-elders,
The learned conversations of the artists:
Young gentlemen, young ladies
In separate chambers shading
With charcoal the beard of Jupiter
And the sunflower breasts of plaster Clyte.
Is it not true that bronzing

The pods of milkweed is more beautiful
Than gilding cat-tails?

Was this the house where
What's-his-name
That railroad builder lived?

You must be thinking of
That millionaire miner
They wouldn't let into the hotel
With his favorite whore
So he bought the hotel
And galloped in on a bronco
And shot down eleven people.
I think it's in some book.

Remembering tomorrow's easier:
Does the jet plane leaving for Paris
On Number 12 North Concourse
Know of the rat at midnight long ago
Creeping the butcher's block of buttonwood?
Was there a lamp-lighter toting his ladder home
When the moon was full, no lamps to light?
Was there a city?

Some ponding of the night is ever on us,
Walking so surely down the street and seeing
Too suddenly the form of what is gone,
And not remembering the form,
Angry at absence,
Cheated by the known,
Aware of always being unaware.

The fretful sly oblivions
Of now
Are on us by surprise.

Cosper Cubic Foot of Up

I'll build me a building forty miles high
And I won't come down 'til the Fourth of July.

CAN'T see you Monday!
CAN'T see you Tuesday!
CAN'T see you Wednesday!
Thursday's tight!
Christ, then make it Monday lunch,
I'll take the figures home tonight.

The architect is working late,
Twitching fingers estimate
How to make forever last
Until a fiscal year has passed.

The architect who didn't know he had to be a PR Man who
didn't know he had to be a taxidermist fitting a glassy skin
to the rib-cage of the newest building higher than the newest
highest building higher than the newest highest building last
time he got his glasses fixed and got married again and got
the poison for the slugs killing the lilacs and got a check-up
from the doctor and got another loan from the bank and got
the newest sports car and got on the list for the newest
country club and got a job promoting the newest highest
building higher than the newest highest building with the
newest highest ear-pop elevators musicking up
to the newest highest cocktail lounge where the
girls droop over the topless mountains honey 'dja
hear about the homo that met up with
the lesbian in Des Moines. ...

The dragonflies have gone to sleep,
Over the city night is still
As the beautiful beautiful long-haired wig
Glued to the skull of Buffalo Bill
Entombed in a thicket of TV towers

And beer-can spruces and kleenex flowers
Up on Lookout Mountain.

Arcturus stings the TV towers,
Punctual spruces ring the hours,
Cambial testaments of frost,
Sunlight captured, snowflake lost,
And bristling under the hogback range,
Where once there twinkled a lamp-lit town,
The city spangles, endless, strange
As the starry heavens upside down.

Night is invoiced out of sight,
Cigarettes and pencil quiver
Cost per cubic foot of up,
Tick-tock eleven,
Tick-tock twelve,
Double-entry beer cans flick
Ashes of arithmetic,
Tick-tock one,
Tick-tock two,
Cosper cubic foot of up,

I'll come to bed in a little while ...
LEAVE ME ALONE! GOD DAMN IT, DARLING!

Cosper cubic foot of up,
Cigarette the coffee cup,
Cosper ton per cosper tax,
Amortize the soggy butt,
Subdivide the cosper cubic
Belly gagging alkaseltzer,
Borrow, borrow
Bank tomorrow. ...

Coming in a minute, dear. ...

Sleeping pills trudge up the stair,
Kissper lacy neverwhere,
Cosper ... cosper ... cos. ...

Drouth—1824

Hear how the wagons crack
In the copper drouth of the prairie,
The pitch that boils from the seams
Is not yet chilled by the moonrise,
The great wheels groan like slaves,
Under the loads they carry,
The wheels are shrunken and spiked
With wedges to keep them from breaking.

The stars are silver and dry
Long past the hour for camping,
Somewhere beyond the midnight
There flows a crystal river,
And thru a hundred wagons
No heart can tell the distance,
But on the toiling oxen
The yoke-irons jingle stronger.

Soon will the oxen drink
Slow rippling moons from the water,
Water that soothes the pain
Of thorn-bruised hoofs and fetlocks,
Water that quenches thirst
Of men and the wheels that bear them,
Water that quiets wheels,
Swelling them tight for the morning.

Elegant Dust

You didn't know you came to make a city,
Nobody knows when a city's going to happen.

You worked your whipsaw shacks up Cherry Creek,
Scurry of silver minnows twitching the sand-burs,
You couldn't tell the soda crust from quicksand,
One boot scuffing solid alkali,
The other hovering a step-off plunge.

Vesper-still as a rustle of thistle-birds
The antelope fell back,
Magpies interlacing cottonwoods,
Zig-zag echoings of black-is-white
And the night could hear
Ox-hide hinges flicking a candle gutter
Of argosies forsworn and rainless seed,
Nicks in the blade of the axe,
The rotting sluices
Panning out prayers no higher than the blow-flies.

Whiskey dripped on quit-claims torn from Bibles,
The white plum blossoms brought the bloody flux,
And there were graves and pimps and nuns and lawyers
And open squaws and opium and lungers.

You didn't know you came to make a city:

You danced by lantern light and a calico moon,
You whisper-kissed the long forever words,
You planted lilacs, rhubarb, sweet alyssum;
You chanted Bethlehem by skift of snow,
You told of Cinderella to the small ones
Going to sleep their first long all-night rain,
The willow leaves so lovely in the morning.

You braided daisies into golden hair,
You picked wild choke-cherries,
You knew of ghosts.
You were courteous to the children of cannibals,
You hatcheted a loco mare in her traces,
You picked the bishop's bedbugs from the mattress,
You were patient with wrinkled cream the thunder soured,
Patient with maggots, patient with all
The knotted idiosyncrasies of hangmen.

You sang together and you read out loud,
Sparrows and churches came,
There was elegant dust
In the socket of the buggy whip on Sunday.

Inscription

>·I·◆>·•·O·•·<◆·I·<

Warriors who sleep
Not one but seven cities deep,
Are singing still,
Stronger than we
Who lie within this hill.

Lovers whose lust
Called ships to sea and men to dust
Are heard above
Our stone-cut names
Where slow brown mosses move.

If you who dare
No more than we in love and war,
Dare faith in fame,
Come when the moon is high
And try to read a name.

Elegy — New Mexico

Row twelve, grave ten,
Block C, Oise-Aisne,
Only the shepherds go to sleep
To songs the shepherds make for sheep,
Sleep, Cosme Gallegos.

Jose Maria Pena,
Six twenty-two D.
Silvio Gonzales,
Eight six C,
Aragon, Carabajal,
Graves, rows, blocks all,
Earth is thick
And grass is thin
On you and Peter Peloquin,
But the pinon trees are much the same
And somebody with another name
Is singing the songs you used to sing
To the other sheep in another spring;
Somebody with another name
Is watching the grass grow into wool
To turn into clothes
To turn into clay,
Somebody with another name
Is going to earth a different way.

The sheep that cry the whole night long
Never will hear the shepherd's song;
Only the shepherds go to sleep
To songs the shepherds make for sheep.

The Empire Sofa

They could grow used to seeing bones
Of buffalo and sometimes men,
They could grow strong on cracking dreams
Of gold to give them rest again,
They could pit happy years to come
Against the prairie's timeless length.
They had illusions that could calm
The frantic restlessness of strength.

But things like this they had to pass,
Sunk in the sand on the Arkansas,
This rosewood sofa that clutched the sun
With every foot a gryphon's claw;
They saw it shining far ahead,
They turned to see it far behind,
And dreamed of men who dared not lose
The things they dared not hope to find.

One wagon whistled *Money Musk*,
Another chattered into laughter,
But no one spoke to anyone
About what they were going after;
An hour creaked by and dreams came back,
The wagons talked with even breath
And grew secure the more they passed
The more familiar forms of death.

Fishing Upstream With My Father

So much spoke to me of your death,
The urn-shaped flowers of mountain heath,
Canyon darkling sallow umber
Shading into autumn slumber,
Yet some deep feel of joy to be
Began to pulse and pulse in me
As I began to wade and talked
To us of river floors we'd walked.

Under that sad but warming sky
I was precise as casting a fly
In where I let your ashes fall
From our Big Rock pool in the canyon wall
To the meadow's undercutting shelf
Where the stream curved back to meet itself
And almost did, each ripple burning
Into foretelling of returning.

I let a bright Gray Hackle whip
A peacock loop from the springing tip
Of my rod and watched it coil, uncoil
Over this now and over all
The nows and nows and nows to come
And the line felt good against my thumb,
And we gave that day to the river more
Of us than it had known before.

Fort Laramie

Skylike grew delphiniums
Through the planking cracks in the two-inch floor;
This is Wyoming walking in,
I said, through an open door.

Wyoming is old as a rotting plank
That is not humus yet,
Blue flowers walk through an open door,
They grow through puncheons in the floor,
Petals blow on the trapper's hearth.
Under this floor and in the earth,
I said, is a taproot net,
And the roof is a thing the sun shines through
To make Wyoming flowers blue.

I touched the frame, there was no door,
It was a place where a door had been;
I said there was a time before
These bluest flowers came walking in
When such a quiet opening
In a strong wall in the afternoon,
With no one here and a strong door gone,
Would have been a fearful thing.

(I said Cheyennes and Sioux left more
Than silent flowers upon a floor.)

I watched the pigeons roar and pound
And drag their tails upon the ground,
And I said these walls are thicker than
The arm's length of a prairie man,
But I said a pigeon circles through
These four white walls of stony mud
As if no smoky pane had ever
Turned the sun to pigeon's blood,

I said does anyone recall
When birds did not fly through this wall?

My hand touched the bud of a blue flower's coming
And I heard a pigeon's mating drumming;
What is Fort Laramie? I said,
There flows the Platte, here are the dead:
They lie in a fold of the greasewood ground,
A few were killed and some were drowned,
And some had reasons for knowing why
Any place was a place to die,
And I looked to see if any stone
Said *Better die here than in Oregon,*
And I looked for letters that could be pieced
Into *We died here on our way back East.*

But I found no words from the honest dead
For the living had marked the stones instead.

Lone men grow honest when they die,
You can sometimes tell by the way they lie
Where they were going and why they stopped,
But these, I said, have all been propped
In cottonwood boxes of compromise
With coppered eyes on paradise
And backs set tight against the world,
With arms well crossed and fingers curled;
How many death-set arms were cracked
To build a sign the living lacked?
How many honest muscles sprung
To fit a hymn that must be sung?
What is a cross upon a breast
That does not face the East or West,
Here under me
At Laramie?

Fort Laramie is Nature now:
I said if there is any trace
Of how many millions passed this place

Under canvas tilts with faces drawn
On the bitter dream of Oregon,
Then any man is natural
As a prairie dog or a coral thing
Or a wind that blows a mountain down.

Bill Sublette was a coral thing,
This is your reef, too, Broken Hand;
Bob Campbell was a prairie dog,
This is your mound of earth, Bob Campbell;
Jim Bridger was a blowing wind,
This is a mountain's bone, Old Gabe;
Kit Carson, did you write a will?
This graveyard, Kit, is also Nature;
Dreamers, fighters, cowards, lovers,
Here is a plank a blossom covers,
Here is Wyoming walking in
With a blue flower and a pigeon's wing.

Fort Vásquez

I've tried it slower but I think it's better
To be going fifty miles an hour or faster
When you pass by those low adobe walls
Builded by Louis Vásquez on the Platte
A hundred years ago. You pass them on
The motor road from Denver to Cheyenne.

This Louis Vásquez led the fur brigades,
He was Jim Bridger's partner many years,
They wandered on these prairies and these mountains:
If you take the skeleton of a cottonwood leaf
And call the stem the long Missouri River
And the other bones of the leaf the other rivers—
The Yellowstone, the River Tongue, the Big Horn,
The Stinking River and the Rosebud River,
The Wind, the Chugwater, the Sweetwater—
That's where they roamed, but one leaf will not hold
Their rivers on the other side of the mountains.

They built their walls the way the beaver did
Of river mud and golden river grasses,
And of these walls this beaver hunter formed,
Three walls are gone. The earth is almost level
Where they stood.
                    The fourth mud wall, no higher than
The barbed-wire fence a rancher built to keep
The people out, still leans upon the wire,
And the windy barbed-wire cuts it like a saw.
A pace away flashes the whirring pavement,
Behind the pavement is the railroad track,
Where fireweed glows against a bank of cinders.

A long-haired buckskin man was Louis Vásquez,
And a handsome man who had driven a coach-and-four. ...

Last night a magpie crossed the hunter's moon,
And I said:
               "There's a feather for you, Louis Vásquez,
To wear in your hair when you walk alone in October,
A feather, if you meet an Arapaho girl
In the yellow cottonwoods."
                                    Those cottonwoods
Were yellow puffs that trundled away as far
As I could see, like yellow tumble-weeds
Piling against the rose and indigo mountains;
But the magpie flew away and the long-haired man
Was dead, and a hundred prairie years were gone,
And I was making only some of the words
That yellow trees and hills have made before.

But getting back to why I like to pass
These crumbling walls at fifty miles an hour:
I nearly always go this way with men
Who have to know some science for their business;
They always tell me things I do not know,
And it's a road I'll want to travel more
Until I'm surer of each curve it's making,
And where the people go who turn at crossroads.

I've passed Fort Vásquez when the telephone poles
Were whipping by at the rhythm of my heart,
And listened to the driver's quiet story
Of fighting colloids in a filter press.
Sometimes we shuffle pairs of chromosomes,
While the mountains slowly turn and change their places.
(Mountains will follow as a new moon will.)
They whisper: *Do not listen to the driver!*
Tell him the old things we are telling you!

And within a bow-shot of where Louis Vásquez
Stretched out his buffalo robes on willow branches,
The whole binomial theorem clattered down

As something that would work all right until
You tried to make its logic alter Nature.

Another time when we were roaring by
To try to help the farmers fight the drouth,
We talked about the way the guard cells work
For photo-synthesis in the blowing leaves
In the barbed-wire fields on either side of the road.
(The barbs are tufted spindles wrapped in fleece
From sheep and clematis that press against them.)
And when the road was blocked by a tide of sheep
We spoke no more of photo-synthesis,
But I thought of the unseen vapors from the sheep
Charging the air with something for the leaves,
Even as dissolution of their bodies
Must charge the earth with something for the roots.

And what is happening is happening
To roots and leaves that split adobe walls.
You dead Arapahoes in the silent meadows,
We spent that wide green summer's day upon
A picture chart showing your prairie sun
Lifting a fountain water from every leaf,
But the syllables and symbols were our own,
And coming home we wandered among planets,
And filled the road with particles of light
That bounced against the car like summer hail.

So goes this road, but when we near these walls
The driver usually says:
                    There's old Fort Vásquez;
Somebody ought to put a marker there!
And someone says:
                    It ought to be restored!
And I'm about to say:
                    How beautiful,
With what you know of earth and air and flesh,

To let these old walls go the way they're going!
Let's bid them godspeed and be on our way!

Or I'm about to say:
> *How might we best*
Unwing a hundred years? How might we now
Reorganize these elements again
With certitude that those who pass this way
Experience alone the works of Vásquez,
And nothing that our different hands have added?
But by the time the driver ends his plea,
Something has come and gone and come again,
And our feet are pressing hard on the floor again,
And talk begins again, perhaps of women.

There's something I am giving up to tell
You this, and if you turn your head away
When I say words like photo-synthesis,
Can I say more than *Are we here or aren't we?*
Shall we turn back? Is there some other road?

O I will not forget the measured sagas
Of older wayfaring across this world,
We'll keep them too. We add to what they are.
If you have time some night I'll sing you a song
About a loping crescent of Cheyennes
Moving under the moon toward Louis Vásquez;
I'll make a song about John Jacob Astor,
And all his warriors fighting in the mountains,
Or a song about a shadow in St. Louis,
A shadow warm with wine and honeysuckle,
And Louis Vásquez stepping out of the shadow
Into the silver laughter of the lovers;
I'll make a song of an island near St. Louis,
And gentlemen shooting each other down
With perfumed ribbons pinned against their hearts —
That will be Nature too, something that rises
Out of the substance of my flesh as sure

As any vapor rising from the sheep,
But that will not be all, for we are here,
And what has happened on this road is ours.

So, of these walls that stood a hundred years
And now are going back to something we
Believe we have begun to understand,
And of the slow feet that made good this road,
And of the beaver hands that made these walls,
I speak new words, to last until they change,
And when my song is lost, if someone says:
It ought to be restored,
                    let someone lift
One handful of this earth and say:
                              It is!

First Hour

>─┤◆>─●─<◆┤─<

They call the mountain Thorodin,
They call the canyon Golden Gate,
They call the graveyard Dory Hill.

You loved to go to Dory Hill,
You scuffed the weeds and read each stone
As if the tangle and neglect
Were yours alone.

We took you there,
We laid you down,
We wept and hurried
Back to town.

Sundown climbed Mount Thorodin
And Thorodin began to dial
The first hour of a long long while.

(Written in remembrance of Marjorie Lois Hagan, Ferril's close friend and personal secretary.)

A Poet for a Father

Anne Ferril Folsom

—•—◇—•—

It should come as no surprise to anyone that my father turned out to be a poet. He was born "maker," the word for poet in archaic Greek. Out of all the things he made in his lifetime, his poems are simply the most beautiful and profound. His urge to build things began very early. A miniature Roman chariot, which he made for his bantam hen when he was seven, was a beautiful little sculpture of scrap tin and wood—a chariot that any small chicken would be proud to pull. (That small banty must have been quite an inspiration to my father. Grandmother described a loop-the-loop track that he built, with a miniature car for this same intrepid little hen to go whirling around in.)

Although he often made practical things—a cedar closet for my mother's winter clothes or a glass-fronted cage for my snakes—he preferred to work on more fanciful projects. When our house was remodeled in the thirties, there was a leftover tunnel in the attic after a wall was dropped from the sloping roof to make a new third floor room. This triangular tunnel ran almost the entire length of the house, and my father used to remark that it was a shame such a perfectly good tunnel was going to waste. He soon located rails from a mine and had four wheels cast to fit the rails. He built a flat car two people could sit on bobsled-fashion and pull themselves along by the rafters through the entire length of the tunnel, which terminated at a small door that looked down on my father's brightly lit study. The tunnel itself was pleasantly dark, except for an occasional first-aid station equipped with a flashlight and a bottle of medicinal whiskey. Halfway down the tunnel was a trap door in the roof equipped with a telescope to look out at the moon over the rooftops. The train was very popular with my parents' party guests but not with the neighbors. The iron wheels made a gigantic roar like a jet engine.

My father had a strong sense of drama, which demonstrated itself later in his prize-winning play ... *And Perhaps Happiness*. One summer when we were at Brookside, he set up a target range across the brook from the main cabin so we could sit on the porch and shoot at a row of tin cans. They were placed on a plank that rested on two rocks. Nobody was very good at hitting the cans, including my father. One morning, we were all having our usual luck, but Father seemed strangely cheerful. When his turn came, he took careful aim and pulled the trigger. There was a loud clang, and *all* of the cans flew high in the air. Even the plank crashed to the ground. He turned to us grinning triumphantly, "Welcome to Honest John's Rifle Range!"

He had rigged a complicated device that connected a huge frying pan to the plank supporting the cans. The frying pan was hung inconspicuously on a tree off to one side. All anybody had to do was hit the enormous pan, and a spring released, which jerked the board away and sent the cans flying. It was a wonderful contraption, but it took "Honest John" at least twenty minutes to reset it for the next performance.

Poets are often described as having the clear, undistorted vision of a child. Sometimes the similarity to a child doesn't stop there. I always felt threatened when my father, under pressure, angrily raised his voice to me. After I was grown up, I once remarked to Charles Van Doren that he was lucky to have such a dignified, gentle father as Mark. Life must have been very peaceful. "You think we didn't throw chairs at our house?" He looked at me in disbelief.

The skin of a poet, of necessity must be thin, otherwise he would be incapable of being pricked by the small nuances and subtleties of human existence that go unnoticed by the rest of us. It stands to reason that irritation comes easily to such a person. I think this accounts for the emotional volatility of poets I have known, and I believe most families would agree that living with a gifted poet is not all moonlight and roses.

My father defined poetry as "the passionate apprehension of experience that runs the whole range from agony to ecstasy, and it is usually overcast with feelings of transitoriness." All his life, I think he felt the pressure of time passing. He found it hard to reconcile the demands of a full-time job at the Great Western Sugar Company with his compelling need to write poems, particularly when eastern editors were hounding him to quit his job and devote himself exclusively to his poetry. When I was little, I remember waking up in the night to hear my father exploding in angry frustration at not having enough time to write. Those scenes made my mother and me unhappy and fearful.

This was going on in the middle of the depression, when my father was the sole supporter of five people: his parents and the three of us. He felt too much responsibility toward us to surrender his paycheck from the Sugar Company for the notoriously insecure income of a writer, especially during the Great Depression. One can only speculate about the kind of poetry he might have written if he had been free from the necessity of staying in one place and supporting us. Perhaps the restraints on him were not such a bad thing. It takes an enormously well-disciplined poet to survive a life of financial security and unlimited freedom to write.

There were other reasons why my father remained in Denver. He seldom spoke of frightening events in his childhood, but there was one he could never forget. When he was five, his mother took him to the Fourth of July Parade. The air was stifling as people packed together in the heat waiting for the parade to start. My grandmother suddenly grew faint and lost consciousness, collapsing directly on top of my father. The child thought his mother was dead, and that he was going to suffocate. The terror of that moment remained with Father all his life.

I believe early experiences contributed an apprehensive side to my father's nature and a lifelong distrust of the unfamiliar. My grandfather, like many a newspaper man, developed a large thirst and spent considerable time touring the bars with fellow journalist, Eugene Field. Occasionally, Grandfather had to be carried home, and it must have been unsettling for a little boy to see his father like that. In later life, even short journeys produced painful anxiety attacks, and as a result, Father preferred to stay close to home, setting the majority of his poems in the familiar landscape he had known since childhood. He had a favorite phrase he used to repeat: "Whatever you need is within ten feet. If only you have the brains to recognize it." I think he applied this principle to his poetry.

My mother's contribution to my father's career was a generous one. She had a rock-solid belief in his talent and his poetry, and in all her years, I never heard her utter a single critical remark about his work. In the beginning of their marriage, her contribution was mainly decorative. She was striking looking, with dark hair and beautiful eyes, and a flair for wearing clothes. She was extremely tall, almost five foot ten, but she moved gracefully, not the least self-conscious about her height.

My mother's wardrobe was both fashionable and mysterious. One day she was approached by a prominent Denver matron whom she hardly knew. Like the good fairy in a fairy tale, the lady promised my mother a closet full of beautiful clothes if Mother never asked where they came from. To my mother's amazement, the woman's driver arrived a few days later with a large box full of expensive and stylish clothing. Everything fit perfectly. It proved to be only the first of many boxes that arrived over a period of years. To this day, we have never found out who Mother's mysterious benefactor was.

In the midst of World War I, Mother graduated from the Dennison University Conservatory of Music. Then, in a burst of patriotism, she enrolled in the School of Nursing at St. Luke's Hospital in Chicago, where she nursed soldiers through the terrible flu epidemic of 1918. After the Armistice, she returned to private life and almost immediately married my father. He brought her to the family home in Denver, where they moved into an apartment that had been remodeled from numerous upstairs bedrooms.

This was not an idyllic arrangement. My mother had no territory she could call her own, and while my grandmother, whom I adored, was both gracious and tactful, she nevertheless felt herself to be the true lady of the house. A full generation separated the tastes of the two women. My mother preferred candlelight, especially at dinner, and there were wall sconces all over our upstairs apartment. Grandmother, on the other hand, found electricity such an exciting new development that the downstairs blazed with hundred-watt bulbs day and night.

My grandfather's small weekly newspaper, *The Rocky Mountain Herald*, was the oldest weekly in Colorado. Revenue came from legal notices, and he published it successfully for many years. Eventually, he became too old to continue, and since my mother was the only available replacement in the family, she agreed to try her hand at managing the paper.

In a short time, it became clear that my mother and the *Herald* were made for one another. When she began to solicit legal advertising from Denver attorneys, they took one look at her and swamped her with their "Notices of Final Settlement." In the beginning they gave her their business because she was beautiful, but they soon discovered that my mother was as accurate and fastidious with her proofreading as she was attractive. Since a misspelled name can tie up a court case indefinitely, her reputation grew quickly, and she soon had doubled the paper's number of clients.

Once she had mastered the paper's routine, she began to introduce a few quirky innovations. The family dog, Mark Van Doren Ferril, turned up on the masthead as "Assistant Editor." Other editorial appointments quickly followed. Her friend Leonard Wibberly, author of *The Mouse That Roared*, became "Sea Serpent Editor." Whenever something piqued mother's curiosity, she would appoint one of her friends as the editor in charge of that subject. She also introduced new columns: my father's extremely successful *Childe Herald* column, and several written by herself, including *Cooking Can Be Fun! by Helene*. This consisted of recipes containing weird instructions and dreadfully incompatible ingredients that seemed oddly plausible until you read them carefully.

Although, in private, my parents often referred to the paper as *The Rocky Mountain Albatross*, they loved the *Herald*. Its front page provided a place where they and many of their writer friends could say whatever was on their minds. Although none of the distinguished contributors ever got paid, no one seemed to care. Two books resulted from the *Herald's* front page: a collection of my father's *Childe Herald* columns called *I Hate Thursday*, published by Harper & Bros. and *The Rocky Mountain Herald Reader* published by Morrow. Mother insisted on a package deal for the *Reader*, in which Morrow agreed to publish a new book of father's poems, *Words for Denver*. In addition, my mother managed to find the time to do the text for the best-selling *Indoor Birdwatcher's Manual*, and its sequels.

I like to think of my father as America's most famous little-known poet. His peers knew far more about him and his poetry than the general public did. Carl Sandburg came to visit us often, prompting my mother to exile me to sleeping on the porch because we had no guest room. She didn't always remember to warn me in advance. Once, I returned from school, threw my books down on my desk, and turned to discover a strange figure spread out on my bed. The head was wrapped mummy-wise, in a long, black silk scarf, and the body was wearing my mother's pale blue negligee. Bony feet stuck out below the negligee, and I could see a man's hand and a big wristwatch protruding from one of the satin sleeves. Sandburg was taking his afternoon nap. My parents must have given him a key, and he had gone to the closet and grabbed the first thing he could find to put on while he napped.

Not every distinguished writer ended up being a fan of my father's. One memorable night Father got a phone call at 11:00 P.M. "This is Bill Saroyan," said a voice. He explained that he was between trains and someone in New York had recommended he look up Tom Ferril if he ever got to Denver. Although Father had had an exhausting day, he invited Saroyan over for a drink. Then he stretched out on the couch to wait for him. When he awoke, fully dressed, the sun was shining brightly. He had a dim memory of hearing the doorbell ringing repeatedly some time during the night, but that was all.

Father made friends from all walks of life. About the only trait they had in common was being extremely good at whatever they did. They could have been a distinguished behavioral scientist at Johns-Hopkins like Curt Richter, or a master stone mason like Posey Lamping, who rebuilt the fireplace at Brookside. Father made friends with many farmers in the course of his work at the Sugar Company. He came to believe that people who worked close to the land had a special dignity and wisdom denied to city dwellers, and he particularly liked the way they used words.

He also had friends in the arts. The paintings in the rotunda of the Colorado State Capitol Building resulted from a cheerful evening my father spent with his close friend Allen True, whose western murals had already gained national prominence. The two of them decided that water should be the subject of Allen's commission, and they sketched out preliminary plans on the paper sack that their hamburgers came in. They decided that Father would write titles and also a poem to go on the wall to complement the murals. I have always been proud to see my father's prescient sonnet on the wall in the rotunda where we held his memorial service as poet laureate.

The lasting quality of my father's work can perhaps best be measured by the numerous people who are willing to make such a concerted effort to keep his writings and his memory alive almost a decade after his death. I, my two daughters, Cameron Olen and Dana Milton, and the other members of the Ferril family would like to express our deep gratitude to all of you who have loved my father and his poetry, and who have worked so hard to make this book possible.

Selected Poems

Tom Ferril introduces goats to the poet Carl Sandburg, seated next to Tom's wife, Helen (1938, Arvada).
Photo credit: Denver Public Library, Western History Department.

Here Is a Land Where Life Is Written in Water

⊱—┼—◆≻—○—≺◆—┼—⊰

*Texts for the Murals by Allen T. True in the
Rotunda of the Colorado State Capitol Building*

Introductory Sonnet
Here is a land where life is written in water,
The West is where the water was and is,
Father and son of old, mother and daughter,
Following rivers up immensities
Of range and desert, thirsting the sundown ever,
Crossing a hill to climb a hill still drier,
Naming tonight a city by some river
A different name from last night's camping fire.

Look to the green within the mountain cup,
Look to the prairie parched for water lack,
Look to the sun that pulls the oceans up,
Look to the cloud that gives the oceans back,
Look to your heart and may your wisdom grow
To power of lightning and to peace of snow.

First panel: Indian worshipping rain
Men shall behold the water in the sky
And count the seasons by the living grasses.

Second panel: fur trappers led by water
Then shall the river namers track the sunset,
Singing the long song to the Shining Mountains.

Third panel: the wagon people reaching water
Here shall the melting peaks renew the oxen,
Here firewood is and here shall men build cities.

Fourth panel: gold released by water
Water shall sluice the gold yellow as leaves
That fall from silver trees on silent hills.

Fifth panel: the desert farmed by water
And men shall fashion glaciers into greenness
And harvest April rivers in the autumn.

Sixth panel: the engineers bring water to the cities
Deep in the earth where roots of willows drank
Shall aqueducts be laid to nourish cities.

Seventh panel: electric power from water power
Water the lightning gave shall give back lightning
And men shall store the lightning for their use.

Eighth panel: for the future
Beyond the sundown is tomorrow's wisdom,
Today is going to be long long ago.

Ghost Town

><—+—<>—•—O—•—<>—+—<

Here was the glint of the blossom rock,
Here Colorado dug the gold
For a sealskin vest and a rope of pearl
And a garter jewel from Amsterdam
And a house of stone with a jig-saw porch
Over the hogbacks under the moon
Out where the prairies are.

Here's where the conifers long ago
When there were conifers cried to the lovers:
>   Dig in the earth for gold while you are young!
Here's where they cut the conifers and ribbed

The mines with conifers that sang no more,
And here they dug the gold and went away,
Here are the empty houses, hollow mountains,
Even the rats, the beetles and the cattle
That used these houses after they were gone
Are gone; the gold is gone,
There's nothing here,
Only the deep mines crying to be filled.

You mines, you yellow throats,
You mountainsides of yellow throats
Where all the trees are gone,
You yellow throats crying a canyon chant:
        Fill what is hollow;
Crying like thunder going home in summer:
        Fill what is hollow in the earth;
Crying deep like old trees long ago:
        Fill what is hollow now the gold is gone;
Crying deep like voices of the timbers,
Conifers blowing, feathered conifers,
Blowing the smell of resin into the rain,
Over the afternoons of timber cutters,
Over the silver axes long ago,
Over the mountains shining wet like whipsaws,
Crying like all the wind that goes away:
        Fill what is hollow,
        Send something down to fill the pits
        Now that the gold is gone;
You mines, you yellow throats,
Cry to the hills, be patient with the hills,
The hills will come, the houses do not answer.

These houses do not answer any cry.
I go from door to door, I wait an hour
Upon a ledge too high to be a street,
Saying from here a man could throw a rock
On any roof in town, but I will wait:

It's time the people came out of their houses
To show each other where the moon is rising;
Moon, do you hear the crying of the mines:
> Fill what is hollow,
> Send down the moonlight?

It's time the people kindled evening fires,
I'll watch the chimneys, then I will go down;
Steeple, why don't you ring a bell?
Why don't you ring a mad high silver bell
Against the crying of the yellow throats?
Wait for me, steeple, I will ring the bell.
> Pull the rope
> Drift, stope,
> Pull a fathom of rock
> And a cord of ore
> From the higher place to fill the lower,
> The Rocky Mountains are falling down,
> Go into any house in town,
> You can hear the dark in the kitchen sing,
> The kitchen floor is a bubbling spring,
> The mountains have sealed like the door of a tomb
> The sliding doors to the dining room;
> Then thump your hand on the parlor wall
> And hear the Rocky Mountains fall,
> Feel the plaster ribs and the paper skin
> Of the Rocky Mountains caving in;
> Pull the rope,
> Drift, stope,
> Pull down the birds out of the air,
> Pull down the dust that's floating where
> The conifers blew the resin rain,
> Pull all the mountains down again,
> Pull the steeple down
> And a cord of ore
> To fill the dark
> On the hollow floor.

I am an animal, I enter houses.
Some of the animals have liked this house:
The first to come and go were men,
Men animals who dreamed of yellow gold,
Then small things came and the cattle came.
The cattle used this room for many years,
The floor is level with the baseboard now,
But probably the ants came first
Before the people went away;
Before the children wore the sill
With stepping in and out to die;
It may have been an afternoon
Before the conifers were dead,
An afternoon when the rain had fallen
And the children were going back to play.
You children going back to play,
Did you ask the things the animals can't ask?
Did you ask what made the mountains glisten blue?
Did you say: "The great wet mountains shine like whipsaws"?
Did you say: "We're here and there's the sun"?
Did you say: "The golden mines are playing
Yellow leapfrog down the hills"?
Did you say: "Think what it would be like
To be way up on the mountain top
And see how beautiful it is
To be where we are now"?

The children made this doorstone look
Like a whetstone worked too hard in the center,
And the ants went out and the wall went out,
And the rats went out and the cattle came,
But they're gone now, all the animals;
If they were here, and all of us together,
What could we say about the gold we dug,
What could we say about this house we used,
What could we say that we could understand?

You men and women, builders of these houses,
You lovers hearing the conifers at night,
You lovers making children for the houses,
Did you say to yourselves when reckoning
The yield of gold per cord of ore,
Running drifts per cord of ore,
Stoping per fathom per cord of ore,
Filling buckets per cord of ore,
Dressing tailings per cord of ore —
You lovers making children in these mountains,
Did you say something animals can't say?
Did you say: "We know why we built these houses"?
Did you say: "We know what the gold is for"?

I cannot tell: you and the gold are gone,
And nearly all the animals are gone;
It seems that after animals are gone,
The green things come to houses and stay longer;
The things with blossoms take an old house down
More quietly than wind, more slow than mountains.
I say I cannot tell, I am alone,
It is too much to be the last one here,
For now I hear only the yellow throats
Of deep mines crying to be filled again
Even with little things like bones of birds,
But I can hear some of the houses crying:

"Which of the animals did use us better?"
And I can hear the mountains falling down
Like thunder going home.

High-Line Ditch

I ride a quiet broncho, mountain bred,
Along a prairie irrigation ditch,
A waterway about as wide as a highroad,
And deep enough, when you were a boy in a tree,
To make you want to start to build a boat,
Larger than any boat you'd ever seen.

To the left when you're riding north along the ditch
Are the Rocky Mountains standing as if some child
Had cut the mountains out of purple cardboard,
And propped them far and cool behind the hayfields.
Some of the mountains are made to look like mountains.
The hayfields and the mountains and the sunflowers
Smell of going away and never coming back.

You can fix your eyes on the wheel of a farmer's windmill,
And as you ride you can roll the flickering wheel
Along the ridgepole of the Rocky Mountains
Until you have to twist your body to see it.

There are cottonwoods on either side of the ditch.
They arch the water with their mingled boughs,
Making a silver tunnel for blue herons
That fly too slowly to be plausible.
The trees are tall. They crowd so close together,
You could almost rattle a stick along their trunks;
And down the darkness of the silver tunnel,
Not magpies, but their after-images
Are painted in dissolving black and white.
You're always looking where a magpie was.
The cottonwoods are trees that would grow too quickly
For an older place. You who have dreamed with oaks

Might find the cottonwoods too insecure.
But it's different if as an inland prairie boy
Who never saw an oak you ever wound
A top string on a newly varnished top
When cotton was flying from all the trees at once
And found the cotton winding into the varnish.
Often, a summer's day would seem like a snowstorm.
A cottonwood out here can be as old
As any city is, and when you sing
A song about the moon, it is a moon
That comes up big behind a cottonwood tree.
A cottonwood was with me when I first
Became aware the word for death meant death.
I remember how it was for I was standing
With my back to a tree in front of a shuttered house
Where a neighbor had died, and I heard the neighbors say
As each would come through the doorway into the sunlight:
"Let me know if there is anything I can do."
I reached my arms behind as far as I could,
And the bark made handles for reaching a little farther.

I tell these things to the moving shoulder blades
Of a quiet horse, my fingers in his mane.
Something the neighbors said is not forgotten,
Nor is it fixed too sharply on the wheel
Of the windmill that I roll across the mountains.

Yet death that I remember is not death,
Nor is a varnished top a varnished top,
Nor even a cottonwood a cottonwood.
Some love there is suspended through them all,
More than I've known, increasing as I move
Into the twilight of a curving path.
At night there comes a different starriness
When you lean back in your saddle and look up
At Cygnus, gallant swan, turning his wings
Across the Milky Way, the cottonwoods,

Over the errors in the township borders,
Over the people trying to love each other.

With Cygnus I've outridden the erosion
Of a hundred hills and I have ridden far
And naked out of earth of time dismantled.
I've galloped over God. I've crossed alone
The terrible threshold of the glittering blackness.
But when you're following the gleaming swan,
It's good to feel some dark weed clutch your stirrup,
The tall marsh elder dragging its pollen across
The starlight on the black arch of your boot.

Into This Hall

Into this hall that is still younger than
Its youngest face there comes another year;
And still there is no looking at the man
Who draws his chair against the table here
At noon, day in, day out, and feeling there
Are more years in him than the day he came;
And we remember but how young they were —
Those men who do not come.

                        Here, then, a name
Is measured less by years than by that flame
Of prejudice, of genius or of wit,
That makes part of each day a happy game ...
That takes each face and makes something of it
That years can touch only if years remember
How flame can burn too clean to leave an ember.

(Written for the Cactus Club in 1928.)

House in Denver

I can remember looking cross-lots from
This house over the evening thistle and
The bee flowers, watching people coming home
From downtown. In the morning I could stand
A long time watching my father disappear
Beyond the sunflowers which you noticed farther
In the morning. Now tall buildings interfere
In piles of shining masonry, but are there
Walls yet to come no more secure than these?
My city has not worn its shadows long
Enough to quiet even prairie bees.
I often hear a droning sunflower song
Dissolving the steel, and mark a thistle turning
A curling wall back when I'm thistle burning.

In the Clearing

Trees are for youth, but stumps for age, he said.
    A tough anvil, a mushroom and a wren
    Are something on a stump ... but tired old men
Are mocked too much by fine old trees that spread
Out green forever in the spring instead
    Of being nearer death a year ... again
    A tree is whimsical, you climb wind when
You dream too much in trees ... and are mislead.

But a stump, boy, every stump's a constant thing,
    Trees mock your growing young, but stumps, half-rotten,
Tell honest years in every seasoned ring,
    And how much of the world you have forgotten;
Stumps are the blocks where men bow to their level,
Counting God's rings, or off to meet the devil.

High Passage

What pure coincidences were the day the bee
Crossed the black river and came floating further West:
An old man felt no symbol streaming o'er his head,
But crushing English roses in his hunting vest
As if the flowers were there, spoke to his dusty son
Of this and that which he had written in his will,
And prattled on of England till the weary boy
Grew fearful of what lay behind each westering hill,
And watched horizons bobbing through the oxen horns,
Like circles screwed against his own identity,
Which thundered in his ears and through the wagon wheels
To roar beneath the silent passage of a bee.

The day the bee flew further West a Blackfoot girl
Laughed when her mother, mumbling of a buffalo bull,
Told of a maid that once a bull had wooed away;
Also that day a Ute boy topped a brown armful
Of wood with a gnarled snow-snake of the winter games,
Which now, in summer calm, could kindle evening fire;
So twilight fell across the world under the bee,
Whose flight sang down to peace, and while the moon rose higher,
The nodding prairie drowsed, for still unmeasured miles
Lay silent in the grass between the fires of those
Who trusting bulls would learn to fear a bee,
And lonely men remembering a droning rose.

Hillbound

Under the shrill cool quivering of mountain stars
He lay in boyish hate: hate for the time-ribbed scars,
The bloodless crags, the stupid flocks, the wanton birds,
Hate for his mountain folk, their ways, their loves, their herds,
The rough-hewn women of their kind, the dew-plumed sage,
Hate for the space about, the endless space, the age;
Nor would he open up his eyes lest he should see
More things to hate: some shaded voice, some mocking tree,
Some dread assurance that the irons of mountain birth
Would chain him hillbound till he ebbed again to earth.
At length, too full of fearing hate for hating more,
He rose, beastlike, and shook as if to fling the roar
Of silence from his heart, and struck a jagged trail,
And climbed the black unraveling thing up to a pale
Old amber height, and stood there in the winged wind,
As he had done long nights before, and let his mind
Dream o'er the blue plain far below and out to where
A glow of checkered city lit the distant air,
And while he watched, the far-off city lights grew dim,
And slowly drew away … and drew away from him,
As they had always drawn away when he had stood
Upon the clutching crag with longing in his blood;
And in that jeweled far-away were burning eyes
Of one much like himself, sweeping his prisoned skies
To see the peaks, rising like keen-edged silver helves,
Splitting and shivering golden moonlight down themselves,
Forever slipping back the more his longing grew,
Vanishing … vanishing into the open blue,
Leaving him hopeless, broken, in the city's clasp,
Like some old withered mandarin, panting to grasp
A snowy blooming girl who meets his gravid glance
With white withdrawal and sweeps on in ghostly dance.

Judging from the Tracks

Man and his watchful spirit lately walked
This misty road … at least the man is sure,
Because he made his tracks so visible,
As if he must have felt they would endure.

There was no lovely demon at his side,
A demon's tracks are beautiful and old,
Nor is it plausible a genius walked
Beside him here, because the prints are cold.

And judging from the tracks, it's doubtful if
A guardian angel moved above his head,
For even thru the mist it can be seen
That he was leading and not being led.

Kenosha Pass

You go in high gear to Kenosha summit:
That turquoise ocean lapping thirty peaks
Is hay now but the buffalo are dead.
The housing of your differential gears
Will break the gentians, but the Utes are dead.

Lens for Plum Blossom

From tree to tree ahead of me
    A thousand blackbirds flutter.
Then wheel their wings in synchrony
    Like blades of a window shutter.

Blackbirds open, blackbirds close
    The snowy woods: my steaming horse
Is breathing frost and swings his nose
    Up the frozen watercourse.

Sundown notches the mountain gap,
    I snatch a twig of cottonwood,
I stare at the sun through amber sap
    That droops from an icy bud.

It isn't like a lens of glass,
    Nothing that I see is clear:
Blur of bud and mountain pass
    Over a horse's ear.

Yet staring so, not budged an inch,
    I feel the white plum blossoms come
To blow against the saddle cinch
    Shuddering winter-numb.

Life After Death

Down heaviness of winter flowers commingled,
Deeper we laid their bodies in the earth
Than storied levels of the living soil;

But I've come quickly home again from all
The many mansions of the coffin people,
Taking, in lieu of prelates, any elm,
The orders of the maples and the beasts,
The separate fragrances of separate flowers,
The prairie wincing in the summer lightning,
The mountains musical with purple timber,
The faces moving into any road,
Faces desiring, faces that remember;
And crowding graveside logic from my mind
To make room for the coat of a sorrel horse
Splitting the sunlight into shaggy rainbows;
And asking for this moment never more
Of any bird than that it cleave the sky.

I have come widely with my spirit over
The tombs of men, of prairies and of mountains:
I can distinguish with a clear precision
The summer bones of winter-frozen steers
From ribs of unicorns and jaws of centaurs;
I've changed no maiden to a mountain aspen,
Though I might take you to a dappled grove
Where graves are old and this is happening.

And I can tell you as a certain thing,
Still while events within our muscles let
Us swing an arm an arc of the horizon,
That you will love me more for having told you
To see what I have seen in natural men,
In elms, in falcons, or in coats of horses;
And I will love you more than beast or rock
Can love you, or the dead can ever love you,
If, with no special memory of this hour,
You say some day, because you have to say it:
        "Remember how it was when we turned our horses
        Out of the dark arroyo into the sunlight?"

Magenta

Once, up in Gilpin County, Colorado,
When a long blue afternoon was standing on end
Like a tombstone sinking into the Rocky Mountains,
I found myself in a town where no one was,
And I noticed an empty woman lying unburied
On a pile of mining machinery over a graveyard.

She was a dressmaker's dummy called Magenta.
I named her that because, all of a sudden,
The peaks turned pink and lavender and purple,
And all the falling houses in the town
Began to smell of rats and pennyroyal.

The town was high and lonely in the mountains;
There was nothing to listen to but the wasting of
The glaciers and a wind that had no trees.
And many houses were gone, only masonry
Of stone foundations tilting over the canyon,
Like hanging gardens where successful rhubarb
Had crossed the kitchen sill and entered the parlor.

The dressmaker's dummy was meant to be like a woman:
There was no head. The breasts and belly were
A cool enamel simulating life.
The hips and thighs were made adjustable,
Encircling and equidistant from
A point within, through which, apparently,
The woman had been screwed to a pedestal,
But the threads were cut and the pedestal was broken.

I propped Magenta into an old ore-bucket,
Which gave her a skirt of iron up to her waist;
And I told a mountain at some distance to
Become her lilac hair and face and neck.

It was the fairest mountain I could find,
And then I said, "Magenta, here we are."

And Magenta said, "Why do you call me Magenta?"
The sky no longer glowed rose-aniline,
So I looked at the town and thought of a different reason.

"Magenta's a mulberry town in Italy,"
I said, and she said, "What a very excellent reason!"
(I said no more though I was prepared to make
A speech a dressmaker's dummy might have relished,
About a naked Empress of France,
And how she held her nightgown at arm's length,
And named the color of her silken nightgown
In honor of the battle of Magenta,
The very year, the very day in June,
This mining camp was started in the mountains.)

The sun was low and I moved to a warmer flange
On the pile of broken mining machinery,
And Magenta said, "it's always afternoon
Up here in the hills, and I think it always was."

"Why always afternoon?" I said, and she answered:

"Mornings were crystal yellow, too hard to see through;
The realness didn't begin until afternoon;
We both are real, but we wouldn't have been this morning
Before the blue came up. It was always so:

Nothing real ever happened in the morning,
The men were always digging for gold in the morning;
They were dreaming deep in the earth, you never saw them,
But afternoons they'd come up to bury their wives."

Magenta stared a moment at the graveyard.

"These women wanted me to be their friend.
I spent my mornings with them making believe.
They'd sit around me talking like far-off brides
Of things beyond the mountains and the mines;
Then they would get down on their knees to me,
Praying with pins and bastings for my sanction.

"Then they would look into mirrors and come back,
They'd look out of the windows and come back,
They'd walk into the kitchen and come back,
They'd scratch the curtains with their fingernails,
As if they were trying to scratch the mountains down,
And be somewhere where there weren't any mountains.

"I wasn't what they wanted, yet I was.
Mornings were never real, but usually
By noon the women died and the men came up
From the bottom of the earth to bury them."

"Those must have been strange days," I said, and I tossed
A cog from a stamp-mill into a yawning shaft.
We listened as it clicked the sides of the mine
And we thought we heard it splash and Magenta said:

"The men would measure in cords the gold they hoped
To find, but the women reckoned by calendars
Of double chins and crow's-feet at the corners
Of their eyes. When they put their china dishes on
The checkered tablecloth they'd say to themselves
'How soon can we go away?' When they made quilts
They'd say to the squares of colored cloth 'How soon?'

"They could remember coming up to the dryness
Of the mountain air in wagons, and setting the wheels
In the river overnight to tighten the spokes;
But by the time they got to the mountains the wheels
Were broken and the women wanted the wagons
To be repaired as soon as possible

For going away again, but the men would cut
The wagons into sluice boxes and stay.

"Each woman had seven children of whom two
Were living, and the two would go to church.
Sometimes the children went to the opera-house
To see the tragedies. They can still remember
The acrobats and buglers between the acts."

I spoke to Magenta of how the graves were sinking,
And Magenta said, "All this is tunneled under;
I think some of these ladies may yet find gold,
Perhaps," she sighed, "for crowns," and she continued:

"Maybe you never saw a miner dig
A grave for a woman he brought across the plains
To die at noon when she was sewing a dress
To make a mirror say she was somebody else."

"I never did," I said, and Magenta said:

"A miner would dig a grave with a pick and shovel
Often a little deeper than necessary,
And poising every shovelful of earth
An instant longer than if he were digging a grave,
And never complaining when he struck a rock;
Then he would finish, glad to have found no color."

I didn't know what to say to that, so I said:

"It's getting dark at approximately the rate
Of one hundred and eighty-six thousand spruces per second,"
And Magenta smiled and said, "Oh, so it is."

And she said, "Up here the men outnumbered women,
But there were always too many women to go around;
I should like to have known the women who did not need me."
She indicated that their skirts were shorter.

"And so should I," I said. "Are they buried here?"

Magenta said, "I think there were hardly any:
They came like far-off brides, they would appear
Each afternoon when the funerals were over.
Some disappeared, some changed into curious songs,
And some of them slowly changed into beautiful mountains."

She pointed to a peak with snowy breasts
Still tipped with fire and said, "The miners named
That mountain Silverheels after a girl
Who never was seen until along toward evening."

"This is an odd coincidence," I said,
"Because I've been using that mountain for your head."

No Mark

➤─┤─◆➤─◦─◀◆─┤─◄

Corn grew where the corn was spilled
In the wreck where Casey Jones was killed,
Scrub-oak grows and sassafrass
Around the shady stone you pass
To show where Stonewall Jackson fell
That Saturday at Chancellorsville,
And soapweed bayonets are steeled
Across the Custer battlefield;
But where you die the sky is black
A little while with cracking flak,
Then ocean closes very still
Above your skull that held our will.

O swing away, white gull, white gull,
Evening star, be beautiful.

Moonset in Bayou Salade

Meadow Larks.
Snow peaks are flowing
Down silver grooves
Into dark tundra
Pitted with hooves.

Out of the drowsing world,
Hoof-packed and frozen,
Something is pulling
Warm flutes by the dozen.

Doubt What You See.
Those are the mountains,
Believe them, they are,
But nobody knows
How far.

Try it with fingers,
Let them extend,
Do they feel blue
At the end?

Numb Harps.
Now turn around,
Touch the horns of the moon,
Pink and brittle,

Feel, they are sharp
As the yucca that pricks
At the ivory bull,

Now touch the ground,
Pull a willow from June,
Bend it a little,

See, 'tis a harp,
Hear how it clicks,
Icily dull.

Morning Star

It is tomorrow now
In this black incredible grass.

The mountains with luminous discipline
Are coming out of the blackness
To take their places one in front of the other.

I know where you are and where the river is.

You are near enough to be a far horizon.
Your body breathing is a silver edge
Of a long black mountain rising and falling slowly
Against the morning and the morning star.

Before we cannot speak again
There will be time to use the morning star
For anything, like brushing it against
A pentstemon,
Or nearly closing the lashes of our lids
As children do to make the star come down.

Or I can say to myself as if I were
A wanderer being asked where he had been
Among the hills: "There was a range of mountains
Once I loved until I could not breathe."

Planet Skin

Planet skin
Is festering pink
Where protoplasm
Learned to think.

Mountains Themselves

Mountains themselves are plausible. You can look
At the ranges one behind the other folding
Into alien blueness with apparent meaning;
But you'll find you need a bird or something that
An old man said when you start to finish a mountain.

A thunderstorm's an early instrument.
I've used a mountain storm for germinating
The grasses down on the prairie and a sickle
Of lightning for harvest quickly, with wrinkled clerks
Down all at once in the city groping with pencils
Into decimals of wheat long after the arc lights
Have come on. I've done it quickly, often before
I've heard the thunder. Or you can wait for the thunder.

Or you can finish a mountain very slowly
With fans of light that mark the equinoxes,
Setting their red dials at the end of always
The same long street their special sundowns need
For remembering which of the front doors on the porches
Show in a year new scars of tacks from which
Were hung the ribboned wreaths of waxen death.

I have kept careful measurements of this
Since boyhood and prefer the slower way.
Some of the hills I've used are nearly finished.

Nocturne at Noon — 1605

>─┤◆├─O─┤◆├─<

Walk quietly, Coyote,
The practical people are coming now
Into the juniper, into the sage arroyos,
Where the smoke is sweeter than anywhere
And the mud is ready for building
The city of Santa Fé.

While the Puritans over in England
Are getting ready to whisper,
There is a way and we will build a ship,
People in motion are looking at the sage
And seeing where the yellow goes in August
In all the violet sage and silver sage
Along the Rio Grande,
Not that they need the yellow on a faring,
But knowing where it is
And what hills are behind it,
As gulls know where an ochre billow beats
On something that is rock.

Coyote, on the silver road of Spain,
Stalk in the noon, the little mice are dozing,
While you are panting, evening comes to Spain,
Darkens the sculptured rats in Tarragona,
Closes the last Sevillian marigold,
Blackens the windows in Our Lady of the Sea,
And the sailors' sheds grow dim in Barcelona.

Be soft, Coyote of the noon,
Far to the east here is an evening that
Is more than many nights:
This evening, for the first time in the world,
Will Shakespeare leads a madman to his heath
Against the wisdom of a patient fool;

This evening, for the first time in the world,
The little hoofs of Don Quixote's nag
Start striking fire from flinty roads of Spain,
A little trot today, some salty grass,
The first star and the last pale cloud are set.
The cloud is over England, Lear is ebbing
Into the northern lightning of the air;
Somewhere there is a storm, my Sancho Panza;
The star is sinking in the Rio Grande,
Where Cradle Flower with teeth white as a beaver's
Laughs at her lover, Medicine of Corn,
Weaving his body through a hoop of osier.

Be still, Coyote in the noon,
You cannot see the sinking of the star
Into the burnt slit of the Rio Grande,
At noon, Coyote, stars are frail as pollen,
But Lope de Vega's gone to bed,
Philip the Third has gone to bed,
And the child Velasquez sucks his thumb
In the blackness of Madrid,
But Will Shakespeare hasn't gone to bed
And over England lightning flashes,
Soft, Coyote, Lear is mumbling
Into the northern wind.

Quick! To the south, Coyote, look!
Is it a rabbit in the noon?

No hare, Coyote, those are ears
Of a mule that comes up the deep arroyo,
Ears in the grass on the edge of the mesa,
Up comes the head, it's the head of a mule;
O soft, Coyote in the noon,
Oñate comes up the deep arroyo,
Rides up the silver road of Spain,
Juan de Oñate's over the edge now,

Stare, Coyote, at Oñate,
Have you seen a peacock plume before?
Or a spur as heavy as two young turkeys?

Still, Coyote, see his face,
For the mud is ready for building now
The palace of Santa Fé,
See the faces red and black behind him,
The practical people are coming now,
The Mother of Christ rides up the mud,
There's another friar on the left,
They're up on the silver sage again,
They see where the yellow is again,
The mud is ready for making walls
Where the smoke is sweeter than anywhere.
Be still, Coyote in the noon,
The practical people come.

Old Maps to Oregon

>—+—◆—O—◆—+—<

Their maps, when they had maps, were charted well
With names stretching two hundred miles or more,
For timid wives to read the night before
The latch-string on the front door slowly fell,
Leaving them, just a moment, staring hard
Against the door, as if a door could close
Tighter the last time than the doors of those
Who had no prairie wagons in the yard.

Although the scrawny legends overlapped
The wilderness with bitter high deceit,
Such wives at dusk could still smile when they came
Within a mile or two of what was mapped,
Dreaming of harbor, while thick oxen feet
Drummed toward some empty place that had a name.

Noted

I have finished winter nearly,
Secretary to the stalks,
Wild blue lettuce, kinghead, yucca,
Sagebrush where my red mare walks.
Noted: sundown hurts a man,
Noted: planets fixed and frozen,
Noted: meeting on the plain
A dead man's cousin.
Noted: magpies need a glade,
Noted: by the time you touch
Any twig or grama blade
You have changed that much.
Noted of a cottonwood:
Hate could crack you down,
War is ever twice as near
As the nearest town;
Noted of a cottonwood:
Love can hold you ever,
Noted: willows tillering
From the frozen river.

Sleeping Longer

The lady is sleeping longer
in her chair.

Sometimes she touches
her long long hair
as if the girl
who wore the hair
were there.

Nothing Is Long Ago

Here in America nothing is long ago:
George Washington was never in Oregon,
He never saw a Flathead woman flop
Her breast across her shoulder to a child,
He never saw the stranded cedar bark
Blow from her salmon thighs like a weaver's thrums.

But it wasn't long:

The corn came quick enough
For Buffalo Bill to eat it out of a can
In a barber shop in a circus tent in London.
You used to see the old man hanging around
The City Desk as if it were a bee tree.

We cut the trees so quick for planting corn,
Your grandfather on the wall had time to push
A lever on a morning-glory trumpet:

The-Ed-dis-son-ree-kaw-ding-awk-kes-straw
with-elephants-with-elephants-with-elephants
to-ride-upon-my-little-Irish-Rose ...

Nothing is long ago when you hear a saw:
It cuts so quick the centuries of pitch
The seasons wrap in rings around a tree,
The trunk will scream in two before your eyes,
Before your lips can move enough to say:

Is it the whine of a soggy witch in Boston?
Is it a cut slave shrieking like a bob-cat?
Is it a woman splitting in Missouri
to give a man child to the Rocky Mountains?

October Aspens

Noon at Evening.
What if the days be short
And night come soon,
See, through the purple dusk, the aspen hill
Is copper noon.

Threshold of Numbers.
As he rests, panting on his axe, the man is less
A man than some worn register of sun and wind,
Rock-boned, pine-lunged, strung taut of sinewed wilderness,
With tunes of storm fringing the furrows of his mind;
His swinging haft and slicing steel, shining with juice,
Have struck through powdery bark, green flesh, brown heart,
Since dawn to build his aspen cords for winter use;
All day he slowly hews the sweet wild trunks apart,
And slowly counts, as much in dreaming rhythm as awake,
The plunging circles of his axe—one … two … three … four,
Or one or five—whate'er it takes to cleave a break,
Humming a phrase he may never have heard before;
Then, counting trunks into small blocks, he loses track
Of all the strokes he numbered as he cut each one;
Yet feels a strange relation stretching idly back
Through all he's cleft and piled to season in the sun;
Just what his biting axe divides and multiplies,
Seems aspen wood and more, seems vague and true and old,
But stays unmeasured when he scans with measuring eyes
Enough cords in equation with the coming cold.

Christmas Trees.
The tall green peaks are Christmas trees,
With yellow aspen candles set
To glow amid dark mysteries
Of gifts unopened yet,

And all the children of the wind
Prowl through to see what they can find.

Told by a Voyageur.
Christ was nailed to an aspen cross,
The aspens are afraid of death,
His lightning soon will strike them down,
They shake and hold their breath.

Pine-Blossom Mountain

Where have they gone ...
My pine-blossom hours?
My wilderness?

Stumps of pines are charred
On this, my mountain
Jet-planes rattle the sky,
Back-pack men and women
Traipse down from their condominiums,
Wait for the traffic light to change,
Then queue up like coffles of slaves
To climb some flinty path
Clattered with tom-tom racket
Of rock cassettes.

Their children pant along behind
in single file,
I've seen them stop and wonder
At a wilted leopard lily,
I've seen them edge around
A furry pasque-flower
Not trampled yet.

Old Men on the Blue

I know a barn in Breckenridge on the Blue,
In Summit County, Colorado, where
A Ford transmission rots upon the wall
Beside an ox-yoke. You can stand inside
The barn and peer like a pack-rat through the logs
And see how summertime looks outdoors, and see
A sleigh with hare-bells ringing under it,
And snowy yarrow drifting over the runners.

How high the mountains are behind the barn
Along toward evening nobody seems to know,
And nobody seems to know how blue they are,
Not even the old men sitting all day long
On a ledge in the shade in front of the general store;
But they watch the gasoline go up and down
In the big glass pump where the white-faced people stop
Who are crossing the Rocky Mountains.

They watch the white-faced people crawl away
Into the hackled fractures of the peaks,
Up where the Mississippi River ends
And the bodies of the frozen dragonflies
Begin to float to the Gulf of California.

The mountain ranges in the evening fill
The sockets of the old men's eyes with blue,
And some of their cheeks are lavender and lilac.
One long day after sunset sunlight poured
Out of the east, from an amber thunderhead,
To make their cheek-bones shine like yellow gold.

The old men do not speak while the pump is running,
But when you drive away you can hear their voices,

Like sounds you hear alone at night in a canyon
When pieces of blackness clatter on pieces of water,
And you think if you didn't have the car in low,
You could overhear what the mountains have never told you.

At night the old men sleep in houses that
Will always have geraniums in the windows.

Progressive Education

Make a map of morning-glories,
    Are the children dressed?
Tell them picture-petal stories
    They like best.

Tablecloth and spoon and milk,
    Lay the petals on the table:
Here's the land where worms make silk,
    Here's the land of Cain and Abel.

Wind the morning-glory stem
    Around the sugar bowl:
Here's the town of Bethlehem,
    Here's the North Pole.

Hurry off to school now, dear,
    Here's your coat and here's your hat,
Here's your quinine, here's your plasma,
    Here's your bayonet.

Thomas Hornsby Ferril— The Life of an American Poet

Stephen J. Leonard

>–·–‹·›–·–O–·–‹·›–·–‹

homas Hornsby Ferril wrote to his friend and fellow writer John Kouwenhoven, January 20, 1978: "Maybe I've told you. One night I was paired off with this ravishing doll and got nowhere so decided to praise her beauty. Something like this: 'How fortunate to be named Mildred: Think of all the glorious women named Mildred—Mildred di Medici, Mildred of Aragon, Mildred Queen of Scots, Mildred the Great of Russia.' "

" 'Gawd! Mister Ferril! You know a lot of history.' "

Mildred the perceptive. Ferril did know a lot of history, much of it picked up from his parents William Columbus Ferril and Alice MacHarg whose family roots reached deep into America's past. They married in 1888 and by 1896 had three children: daughters Lucy and Harriet, and on February 25, 1896, son Thomas Hornsby.

"As a child," Tom recalled four decades later, "I got so tired of hearing my father talk about the border-ruffian West of the Civil War that I found my-self resisting all concepts of the West." Yet as a poet and essayist Ferril feasted upon history, particularly that of the West, adding to it his own experiences, which he captured with keen eyes and ears, and an equally sharp mind.

By the age of ten, Tom had seen Denver's cable cars replaced by trolleys and was beginning to notice a few automobiles. "The first machines on our block were a Grout and a Yale. Two neighbors of mechanical bent spent all their time trying to make them run." Shortly before his fourteenth birthday, Tom and fifty thousand others—nearly a quarter of the city's population—thronged Overland Park in South Denver to watch the Frenchman, Louis Paulhan, bundled up and wearing goggles, do what no one had done before in Denver—fly. "It was," wrote Ferril, "as if some troubled swamp bird had rustled into the air and fluttered back."

Tom's more down-to-earth routine usually centered on the family home at 2123 Downing Street, the house of his mother's Aunt Joanna, where the Ferrils moved to in 1900. There he mastered the mandolin. There he re-mained for the next 88 years apparently having married the place by perfect-ing "Home Sweet Home" as his first mandolin piece. In the summers the Ferrils sometimes escaped the city by going up Platte Canyon to the MacHarg cabin "Brookside" near Bailey via the Colorado and Southern Railroad. Oc-casionally Will Ferril, who in 1896 became curator of the Colorado Historical and Natural History Society, wrangled free rail passes so his family could accompany him as he gathered specimens for his collections. Those perks ended in 1910 when Will was forced out of his curatorship.

The year Tom's father lost his job, Tom started high school at East Denver Latin School. "We all took Latin, most of us took German and, of course, there was rigorous emphasis on English, algebra, and history. ... no survey courses, no pasting up of scrapbooks on current events and no courses on good citizenship." Despite two hours of homework each night, he ran on the track team, wrote for the school paper, delivered newspapers to Capitol Hill mansions in the morning and to saloons and brothels in the afternoon. At his high school graduation he listened to principal William Smiley assure the class of 1914 that "the world had outgrown war." A few weeks later "a pistol cracked at Sarajevo and the twentieth century began."

By the time the United States entered World War I in April 1917, Tom was a junior at Colorado College in Colorado Springs. There he enjoyed the tutelage of professors such as Homer E. Woodbridge in the English department and the inspiration of visiting lecturers including the English poet Alfred Noyes: "He was the first poet I ever saw or heard ... the entire student body was on hand to hear him read 'The Highwayman.'"

Ferril led a hectic life. He ran cross-country races and contributed an eclectic, chatty column to the college paper entitled "Line Plunges." To support himself he delivered milk from 4:00 to 8:00 A.M., took work with his Phi Delta Theta fraternity brothers as a paid pallbearer, and covered half of his meal expenses by playing the mandolin. He joined the U.S. Army as a cadet and studied radio telegraphy. In April 1918 he was called to active duty at the Radio Training School in Austin, Texas. Commissioned a second lieutenant, he went to New York City where he "gave lectures about radio I didn't understand." He was sitting in the radio room of Columbia University on November 11, 1918, when his wireless told him that the war to end all wars had ended.

Educated and unemployed he returned to Denver where his muse landed him a job. Years later he summarized his early literary career: "I began making poems in my very early years. By the time I was four or five years old, I had made up rhymes about a turtle, a rocking chair and other immortal subjects. From five to seven I went into a slump. Maybe I was burnt out. ... But soon the divine fire was rekindled. At nine my first poem was published." He continued to write at Colorado College and in the army. Will Ferril, who in 1912 had purchased the *Rocky Mountain Herald*, a small circulation weekly, proudly ran his son's pieces signed "Thomas Hornsby Ferril." Arthur Chapman, managing editor of the *Denver Times*, liked poets. In early 1919 he made Ferril a reporter at $15 a week. Tom wore his army uniform until he could afford a suit.

He took the assignments that came his way: watching the police torture a feeble-minded prisoner one day, on another writing of "the greatest electrical development of the decade," the wonderful new vacuum tube. He interviewed the greats of the era, including U.S. Army General John Pershing and movie idol Mary Garden. Opera star Enrico Caruso, having gotten a callous on his hand from signing pictures, asked Tom: "Is that what you call a corn?" "Not," replied Ferril, "unless you walk on your hands."

For an extra $10 he wrote entertainment columns in which he attacked "stupid and trashy" films and jabbed at "erotic mush" and the "soft-chinned men and the ox-eyed flappers whom the public has been taught to recognize as movie stars." Theater owners fumed until they paid him $60 a week to work for them. Beginning in November 1922 he tweaked that income by writing a weekly Sunday poem for the *Rocky Mountain News*. By December 1925 when the paper pruned paid poetry Ferril had produced more than a hundred verses. With poems at $5 each he earned enough to buy a grand piano, symbolically reinforcing the union between poetry and music that characterized his work.

During those years Ferril faced the choices that poet Robert Frost described when he wrote of two roads diverging in a yellow wood. Tom might have followed the lead of other talented writers: Gene Fowler, Damon Runyon, Katherine Anne Porter, and his boyhood friend George Willison, who abandoned Denver. Even his boss Arthur Chapman, famous for his verse "Out Where the West Begins," went East. Tom may have considered doing so himself. An acquaintance urged him to try his luck in New York City: "You can sleep in my apartment if you like and save hotel bills."

Instead he married Helen Ray in Newark, Ohio, on October 5, 1921, with George Willison serving as his best man. Tom brought Helen home to the Ferril house where they occupied the second floor while Tom's parents lived below. On August 12, 1922, Helen and Tom's daughter, Anne, was born.

With his family and location set, he remained unsure of his career. He knew he could not make a living by writing poetry. He could as a journalist, but he did not like the "miserable Denver sheets." He considered an academic career, but lacked advanced degrees and did not want to teach freshman composition. University of Colorado President George Norlin politely discouraged him: "We're kind of running an assembly line now and we've got to move these people along whether we like it or not."

His friend William Lippitt, General Manager of Great Western Sugar, helped him escape from the theater business in 1926 by hiring him as a press agent. Ferril later joked that he spent "part of my time working for the Great Western Sugar Company and part of my time writing poetry." In fact, he worked full time for the company, editing its magazines, planning its advertising, making its movies, writing speeches for its officers, and preparing its annual reports. "I never regretted a minute that I worked for the company, because it was a fascinating university in itself."

He met the elite. With Great Western's President William Petrikin, Tom visited President Herbert Hoover who raised and lowered a window shade to illustrate the rise and fall of tariffs. The shade crashed to the floor. Farmers could also be fun. "Poetry" said Ferril, "is a very passionate apprehension of experience, which is always stated in concrete symbols." Farmers pleased him with vivid language. "Pure tiger shit" one happy grower proclaimed as he showed Tom his rich land.

Tom somehow found time to do everything else: raise and race pigeons, fish, remodel, write, teach, entertain, and support his family, including his parents. He walked his dogs, who were also family; corresponded with friends, fans, critics, publishers; published tens of thousands of words of prose, and wrote hundreds of poems. Such a supersaturated life sometimes drove him and those around him nearly mad. "I can't plan" he often impatiently told his daughter, who eventually recognized his need to leave time free so he would have some for himself. He remembered the pressure in the mid-1940s when he was writing a column for *Harper's* magazine: "I would get up at maybe four-thirty or five in the morning and work right through until about maybe ten. Eat, rest, get piece to the airport by 2:30. You didn't have much time to revise." He confessed to one publisher: "A divided life like mine has to have a number of angles that have to dovetail if it is to make sense—and I often wonder if it does."

He put a high priority on writing poetry. "You can't take up poetry the way you would take up archery or selling insurance or deciding to start a hot dog franchise. It's something that's a commitment." Tom recognized that poetry, like his pipe and cigarettes, was not something he could put down. "Poetry is something you are stuck with. You've got to do it whether you want to or not." Two things, he said, are worth living for, "fishing and poetry, and in winter you can't fish."

In 1922 Frank P. Davis published two of Tom's newspaper verses, "From a Coyote Primer" and "Hillbound," in *Anthology of Newspaper Verse for 1921*. Richard LeGallienne, a critic for *The New York Times*, was so impressed with "Hillbound" that he reprinted it in the *Times*. "Denver," he said "very evidently owns a poet, who, as the phrase goes, will bear watching." The watching bore fruit in 1926 when Ferril won the Yale University Press young poets competition, an honor accompanied by Yale's publication of *High Passage*, his first book of poetry. *The Nation* magazine iced his cake by naming "This Foreman" its top poem in 1927. The same year he won second prize in the "Spirit of St. Louis" contest for "The Arrow of Acestes." Homer Woodbridge, his former English teacher, congratulated him: "I am proud of you, of course, and none the less because I haven't the slightest notion what 'This Foreman' is about."

Ferril would explain events that triggered a poem. He noted that "This Foreman" sprang from the death of a construction worker he had witnessed. "Cadetta-C&S" had its roots, Tom told school children, in his own childhood when he saw a coffin being loaded on a train. But he almost always refused to translate even small parts of his poetry into prose. He argued: "to try to describe a poem, or say what a poem says in words other than the poet employed, conjures up that sad dilemma of our early schooling when the teacher would ask us to put Macbeth's 'tomorrow and tomorrow' into our own words. Might as well ask a boy to change a John Deere tractor into a dugong."

Tom mastered the art of writing short poems. But occasionally his genius prodded him to write a long piece and then he sometimes had to argue with editors who preferred short submissions. Bernard DeVoto asked him to send some work to *The Saturday Review of Literature*. "For the sake of my managing editor's frayed nerves, let us momentarily assume that poetry ends with the thirtieth line." In 1936 a more tolerant Robert Penn Warren of *The Southern Review* published "This Lake is Mine," which Tom described as "a long water poem ... about a little lake in City Park, Denver, but that doesn't prevent my dragging in everybody from Sam Hearne to Bill Williams." Initially he sent "Words for Leadville" to *Esquire* magazine, which requested that he trim it. He refused and submitted it to Harriet Monroe of *Poetry: A Magazine of Verse*. She found parts of it shocking, but Ferril refused to make changes so she published it in its entirety in 1936.

Ferril reacted angrily to criticism he considered unfair. Marian Castleman, a reviewer for *Poetry*, faulted him in 1944 for not being sufficiently contemporary. He responded: "Miss Castleman would like me 'to come to grips with Today.' I have never done anything else; moreover my today is not one-dimensional." He also disliked dullards' praise. "I do think to be praised by a bad critic kind of gives you goose flesh." Ferril also feared well-meaning people who touted him as their regional poet. He may have promoted that thinking himself by titling his second poetry collection *Westering*, which Yale published in 1934. His third poetry book appeared in 1944 bearing the nonlocal title *Trial by Time* and in 1952 *Harper's* issued *New and Selected Poems*. "It is better," Tom wrote Ramona Herdman of *Harper's*, "to mention me as an American poet who lives in the West. Or a Western American poet. The regional emphasis so often results in the local-boy-got-a-poem-accepted sort of thing, and I always wince and get itches, when some kind chairman introduces me as 'the poet laureate of Colorado.'"

By the time *New and Selected Poems* appeared, Ferril the essayist was as well-known as Ferril the poet. "I had a deep-seated aversion to any kind of prose writing," he wrote in 1966. "My commitment was, as it is now and will be henceforth, to poetry." That attitude notwithstanding, Ferril produced reams of remarkable prose. As a young reporter he saw his account of the conversion of Denver's Tabor Opera House into a movie theater published in *The New York Times*. In the 1940s he wrote regular columns for *Harper's* magazine getting $350 per article for "Western Half-Acre," a generous sum compared to the $125 *Harper's* paid him in 1939 for the long poem "Harper's Ferry Floating Away" or the 88¢ in *High Passage* royalties Yale credited him with in 1930.

He made his most significant prose contributions as "Childe Herald," a columnist from 1939 to 1972 for *The Rocky Mountain Herald*. Founded in 1860, the paper billed itself as the oldest weekly in Colorado, although Tom admitted that it had died in 1864 and been reborn in 1868. Will Ferril purchased it in 1912. As Will's eyesight gradually deteriorated in the 1930s, Tom's wife Helen, known to friends as Hellie, took charge of the paper. In 1946 Tom compiled edited versions of his columns into a book, *I Hate Thursday*, with drawings by his daughter, Anne Ferril Folsom. He hated Thursdays, he explained, because of the deadlines he faced that day. In 1966 Helen and Tom jointly produced *The Rocky Mountain Herald Reader*, which included Helen's witty columns and recipes as well as Childe Herald's essays.

Whether in the *Herald* or in *Harper's*, in book reviews or in private correspondence, Ferril used prose, as he did poetry, to air his thoughts, to express his humor and his pain, to reminisce, plumb truth, ponder beauty, to understand time, mountains, water, life, death, to brush off fools, to smite his enemies and sometimes his friends. A Republican in an era often dominated by Democrats, he was ever anxious to set the country right. Tom was antiwar, anticensorship, antigrowth, antiurban renewal, antitourism. When his nation, state, and city tolerated and even favored war, censorship, growth, and demolition, he needed some place to let off steam.

Ferril was the epitome of a bundle of contradictions: religious, but without a conventional creed; sensitive to rejection, but often risking it; normally healthy, but given to hypochondria. A man of modest means, he associated with the rich and famous. The pigeons he raised for racing could, he thought, be used to feed his dinner guests, but often the birds lived because he could not bear to kill them. He damned conformity, but worked for the same company for 42 years and lived in the same house for 88. Charming and cantankerous, shy and boastful, leading an overcrowded industrial and literary life, Thomas Hornsby Ferril needed a therapist. He found one in his Underwood typewriter.

His prose mirrored his nature: kind, whimsical, nostalgic, angry, sarcastic, waspish. In a 1941 *New York Herald Tribune* review he roasted *Colorado: A Guide to the Highest State*. "The book is riddled with error, clumsily organized, badly indexed and the maps are downright wretched." George Willison, Tom's boyhood pal, who edited the federally funded guidebook, responded "you are full of condensed billy goat pee." Tom shot back: "All I can say is to hell with you." George backed off and Tom apologized. Five years later when Ferril's *I Hate Thursday* got a bad review Willison comforted him and made a point at the same time: "God damn those pip-squeaks who can make or break a book, and it doesn't take them ten minutes time. ... To hell with them."

Tom knew the value of connections and he treasured his associations with other writers. Through his participation in summer writers' conferences at the University of Colorado in the 1930s and 1940s he made friends with such renown novelists as Thomas Wolfe. His and Helen's hospitality also helped. They treated Wolfe to a two-day tour ranging from Central City to Colorado Springs in the summer of 1935. Once, thoughtlessly, Tom encouraged the 300-pound Wolfe to sit in Anne Ferril's little dog cart. He broke the axle. "I never read *Look Homeward Angel*," said Anne, still miffed years later.

Ferril used his father as bait to hook the poet Carl Sandburg, who was working on a biography of Abraham Lincoln: "Next time you come to Denver, if it is your will, I will hide you from the public gaze in the back bedroom. … You can talk to Dad about the border-ruffian days in Kansas." Sandburg stayed with Helen and Tom often enough to later admit: "Yes, it's quite a board bill I've run up with the Ferrils." He paid part of that bill by praising Tom: "He is the poet of the Rockies, and someday he will be recognized as one of the great poets of America." Robert Frost, who ranked with Sandburg among the nation's best-known literary figures, also visited in the 1930s, drawn to Colorado to see his daughter Marjorie in a Boulder sanatorium.

Tom asked his visitors to sign his guest board which mapped the range of his activities and connections. The poets John Ciardi, who the Ferrils befriended during World War II when Ciardi was stationed at Denver's Lowry Field, signed, as did historian Mari Sandoz, who got to know the Ferrils when she lived in Denver. A good number of local literati inscribed their names: Bill Barrett, William McLeod Raine, Caroline Bancroft, Robert Perkin. Civic leader Anne Evans signed. She with Tom and others helped fan embers of Colorado history into a small fire during the 1930s by reviving Central City as a summer cultural center. Novelist Harold L. Davis put his name down twice perhaps because he was one of Ferril's closest long-distance buddies, often exchanging witty letters with him and occasionally writing for *The Rocky Mountain Herald*.

Pulitzer prize winner Bernard DeVoto, another devotee, did the Ferrils no favor in 1952 by publicly praising Tom and his Childe Herald column: "He has never written a mediocre piece; I can't remember even a sloppy paragraph. It is so by far the best weekly column in contemporary journalism that there is no second place; the runner-up comes in third." Subscribers flocked to the *Herald*, which made its income publishing local legal notices and did not want the expense of a big mailing list. Helen politely returned the newcomers' money. She, Tom, and Anne, however, were pleased with the popular success during the 1950s of Helen and Anne's hilarious *Indoor Bird Watcher's Manuals*.

The fifties also brought Tom brief national television stardom as he appeared at Red Rocks Amphitheater in 1956 reading a few lines from his poem "Words for Time" as part of Cecil Effinger's composition "Symphony for Chorus and Orchestra." The next year his blank verse play, "… *And Perhaps Happiness*," won a $10,000 prize from *The Denver Post* and was produced at Central City in 1958. Most importantly, for his happiness, in the early 1950s he employed a University of Denver student, Ichiro Ogawa, to help around the house. From then until the end of Ferril's life, Ichiro took care of him with unflagging loyalty.

For Helen and Tom the 1960s were mixed. The decade started auspiciously with Tom winning the $1,000 Robert Frost Poetry Award for "Cadetta-C&S." The University of Colorado, which brushed him off in the 1920s, gave him an honorary doctorate in 1960, gilding his academic lily since he already had three other honorary degrees. The same year Robert F. Richards, a professor at the University of Denver, did Tom an even greater favor by authoring an excellent Columbia University doctoral dissertation entitled "The Poetry of Thomas Hornsby Ferril." Richards also contributed the insightful foreword to Ferril's fourth collection of poetry, *Words for Denver and Other Poems* (1966), which included "Horn of Flowers," a poem Steuben Glass had selected in 1963 for artistic interpretation in glass.

Tom's strongest link with his boyhood and the nineteenth century snapped in 1962 with the death of his mother at the age of 95. His 42-year association with Great Western Sugar ended in May 1968 when he retired at age 72, forced out, as he put it, "on the grounds of compulsory senility." By then the *Herald* was becoming a burdensome albatross. Helen was hospitalized in April 1968 as a result of a stroke, one of a number to follow. In early August 1972, Tom wrote a gracious obituary for his friend George Willison in the *Herald* and later that same month the Ferrils sold the paper to Clé Cervi Symons, daughter of Denver journalist Gene Cervi. She passed it to Maurice Mitchell, chancellor of the University of Denver, who let it languish. Tom complained in 1976: "He kept reprinting Hellie's and my pieces — then let the *Herald* pass out. He didn't know how to run the paper. Rest in Peace RMH."

On February 22, 1978, shortly before Tom's 82nd birthday, Hellie found her own peaceful rest. Both her last years and his were made more comfortable by a legacy Tom received from his mother's sister, Susan MacHarg, who died in 1967. Among other things the money allowed him to dredge out a little pond at his cabin. He also had the satisfaction of seeing his prose and poetry reprinted and recycled. In 1972 June and Joey Favre of the Third Eye Theater produced "Ferril, etc." a two-hour stage show derived from Tom's works. In 1975 the presentation was shortened for KRMA television, and in 1988 it was revised by June Favre and presented at Germinal Stage by director Ed Baierlein. Tom also stuck to poetry. Named Colorado's Centennial-Bicentennial poet in 1976 he produced the long, historical poem "Stories of Three Summers." *Anvil of Roses*, his last poetry collection, appeared in 1983.

He took time for fun. He socialized at the Cactus Club, the Denver Press Club, the Denver Posse of the Westerners, and the Evil Companions Club, a loose organization where he found admittedly depraved journalists ready to listen to his limericks. He maintained his tradition of falsely claiming that by coincidence it was also his birthday whenever he gave talks, which he disliked, or received awards, which he usually liked. That trick, he boasted, fooled gullible people into giving him gifts.

If that weren't enough, every so often some group would heap an honor on him. The Sertoma Club put his name on a plaque at Tremont Place and Broadway in 1971. The Denver Landmark Preservation Commission, of which he was a member, designated his house a landmark in 1973. His poem "Two Rivers," was inscribed on a tablet at the confluence of Cherry Creek and the South Platte. The National Cowboy Hall of Fame gave him its Trustee's Award in 1983. The same year the Denver Press Club named him "Outstanding Colorado Communicator," and in 1986 it dedicated a table to him. In 1985 he received the Helen Black Arts and Letters Award and donated the $3,500 prize to the Western History Department of the Denver Public Library which also eventually received his papers.

In early 1979, he read poetry at the inauguration of Richard Lamm as Colorado's governor. Afterward Tom, in his impish way, slipped into the capitol rotunda and with a felt-tipped pen signed the verses that he had written nearly forty years earlier to accompany Allen True's murals. Lamm evidently regarded the offense as less than capital for on October 2, 1979, he named Ferril the state's poet laureate. This "local-boy-got-a-poem-accepted" honor, coming late in his career, did him little harm. In the early 1980s, thanks to the half-hour KRMA Channel 6 television documentary "One Mile Five Foot Ten" written by Marilyn Griggs, directed by Don Kinney, and narrated by Gene Amole, Tom's stature was made manifest to Public Broadcasting System viewers locally and across the country.

His daughter Anne and her children Dana Milton and Cameron Olen and a raft of friends piloted by Jane and Tom Cooper as well as by Chris and Robert Richards helped make his last years as comfortable as possible. Ichiro Ogawa and his wife Fumie attended to Tom's needs as did health aide Linda Artz. And from time to time Denver writers and media luminaries including Gene Amole, Tom Gavin, Marilyn Griggs, Bill Hornby, and Jack Kisling reintroduced him to the public.

Tom continued to correspond with his sister Lucy Ela in Grand Junction, Colorado, who, although six years his senior, was destined to outlive him. His other sister Harriet had died in 1935 and many of his long-term friends had predeceased him. Robert Frost, Carl Sandburg, Harold L. Davis, George Willison—all were gone by the early 1970s. Tom wrote his friend John Kouwenhoven in 1979: "Every so often, when my gut growls, it's the end of the world, but if I get a good rest, keep on smoking and drinking, take walks with my dog, etc., these anxieties fade away and I have to dream up new ones." Suffering from poor eyesight and emphysema, Tom's health slowly declined, and at age the age of 92 he died at his home on Friday, October 28, 1988. His last duchess, a Scotch terrier named Sue, joined him two weeks later.

Selected Poems

Report of My Strange Encounter
With Lily Bull-Domingo

If you want to know where it was,
I stopped my car
On the hump of Hardscrabble Pass up Hardscrabble Creek
To stare across the blue Wet Mountain Valley
And listen to the far-off sawtooth snag
Of the Sangre de Cristo Mountains ripping slabs
Of purple from the sky and letting them fall
All purple over purple long ago.

Off there—Rosita, Querida, Silver Cliff,
So old the ghosts were gone but here, as if
I were my very self and she herself,
Stood fair and lovely Lily Bull-Domingo.

Lily leaned against the car
And asked me why I tried to dream
Up words to fit the teeth of peaks
That seemed to slit the sky;
"It never never works," she said,
"I've seen a thousand try,
I've been here nigh a hundred years;
It's simpler doing fishes' tears
Or words for breath of birds."

Lily was young and fresh as a daisy,
Lily was old and cracked and crazy,
Lily was a madam on a stud paint-horse
Chirping like a chipmunk in a watercourse.

"How can you be three different things?" I said;
Lily replied: "It's easy when you're dead,"
And wove three horse-hair halos
And hung them on her head.

I stared at the Sangre de Cristos,
They brought me home to God,
But Lily chucked me under the chin
With a spray of goldenrod,
And Lily asked me why I'd come
And what I'd hoped to find;
"I've come to this lovely valley
In quest of peace of mind,
I want to wander these lost towns
Where not a house still stands ..."

"And talk to ghosts?" said Lily,
"It's possibly your glands,
It might be good for you to try
A laying on of hands,"
And Lily winked and pranced and showed
Her can-can garter bands.

"The woods were God's first temples,"
I said, "Don't break the spell!"
And Lily Bull-Domingo said
That she was sorry as hell
If what she'd said upset me
And asked what my business was:
"Insurance or electronics?
Or maybe you peddle booze?"

I was so stunned, the mountains fell,
The sky was gone, I felt unwell,
I gasped: "Please leave me, Lily!"
"O.K. Bud, if you choose,
But you're plumb fagged out and hungry,
Lay down, take off your shoes!"

My throat was numb, I could not talk,
I felt like a wounded haggard hawk,
She pillowed my head on a granite rock
As soft as eiderdown,
And Lily made soap from grease and ashes,

She washed my face
And kissed my lashes
As if I were her own.

She cut a jag of juniper
And rubbed two sticks to make a fire,
Then Lily dynamited trout
Out of a reservoir,
And Lily bumped a can of cream
Across a mountain range and back,
I marveled how the butter lumped
And how she sizzled up a stack
Of flapjacks and how Lily found
A jug somewhere and how she laughed
As Lily poured the whiskey
And toasted: "Down the shaft!"

We lay on our backs, the moon came out,
My fingers touched her silken thigh,
So I sat up straight and tried to trace
The moonlight down the sky,
Down,
        down,
                to a long-gone town ...
"Is that Rosita over there?"
She sweetly whispered: "Tell me why
e equals mc square."

"Good Lord!" I stormed. "It's mc squared!
But you are not supposed to know
Such things! Now, Lily, get this straight!
You lived a hundred years ago!"

"Then put your hand back where it was!"
"Why should I?"
"Just because ..."

"The night is beautiful," I said,
And Lily said: "Let's make up rhymes:
The twinkling stars, the murmuring breeze,

The pretty columbines … "
"No, no!" I said, "Now stop! You hear?"
And Lily purred: "O.K., my dear,"
And snuggled up and kissed my ear.

"What was it like? I want to know,
Up here a hundred years ago?"

And Lily answered plaintively:
"Let's restore the gallows tree
Over the dump of the North Star mine
And make a killing, you and me,
With a new school of design."

I was so shocked I fell asleep
While Lily chattered endlessly,
I dreamed of Union Carbide,
I dreamed of AT&T,
But through it all I seemed to hear
Lily saying to me:

"And let's restore the pesthouse
And move a symphony in,
And rearrange the slaughterhouse
For cello and violin.

"Let's bulldoze out five parking lots
With lights for *Stop* and *Go,*
And put up neon billboards saying
Watch our ghost town grow!

"And let's restore the whorehouse
with costumed wax-work whores
And let the girls from the Junior League
Give two-dollar guided tours."

Next morning when the sun was up
I knew that this had been a dream
But Lily brought my coffee cup
And ham and eggs and cream.

And Lily, as we bade farewell,
Said: "Maybe we will have a child …
As live as me … as dead as you,"
She smiled and walked and turned and smiled
And turned and walked and walked and turned
As if I were a looking glass,
Then Lily waited for a car
Just coming up Hardscrabble Pass.

I drove down to Rosita
And moped a thousand years
Among the graves in the graveyard
And this brought me to tears:

Lily Bull-Domingo
Died at the age of six,
One, two,
Buckle your shoe,
And save your candle wicks.

Science Came West

They weren't all fighting men, some traded knives,
Tobacco, scarlet cloth, vermillion dye,
And rum and cakes of salt … and some their lives
For aster pollen and a butterfly,
Or for a star against a mountain sky
That fixed the longitude and latitude
Into a crumpled note-book carried by
A thirsty mule that crumpling would be food;
They weren't all fighting men, some gave their blood
To christen wormwood after Artemis,
To pole a perogue through a stinking flood,
To watch a warbler in the clematis …
Now cutting blossoms, now dead manes and tails
For girths to bind fresh horses to the trails.

Reprise

City of mine,
How often in the evening
Have I returned a long long time from now
To sift your shards and middens
From slag of elder wars
And powdered mountains.

I beckon back some ghost who was my friend
And speak to him as if we were alive:
Remember, Tip, here's where the river was,
Remember?

Or turning from the ashes of lost waters,
I listen for what must have been a tree
Before the trees gave way to roaring treadmills
And we by vaporous innocence
Of our own unnatural substance
Changed into going nowhere nowhere faster.

Tonight, Tip, I can't even find
Where Beason's apple orchard was,
There's nothing but these skulls of towers,
What were they, Tip?
Crypts of sky for tick-tock generations
Too nimbly cloyed with plenitude a while
To know the finger feeling of the earth?

Once there were mallow petals to touch in spring
And we could cipher sundown slipping south
By golden rabbitbrush, remember, Tip?
And why, Tip, did they leave no shack or shrine
By ember visitation of their fathers?

It's time, Tip, to be going back
To where we are or are not anything,

But never the same way home:
Let's shag off zig-zag crosslots
From Mr. Bussey's store
Up Grasshopper Hill,
Then mosey on out Dry Creek …

Whereaway?
By benchmarks of old seas?
By Alban snows? By Argolis?
Comparing flavors of manna from tamarisk
With spruce gum that we used to chew
In Carl's backyard before Carl went to sleep
And didn't wake?
I think I hear a plowman singing his Egypt,
Twelve forevers going on and on
By grace of red grain ale
And white white barley.

Yet now, Tip, ere we turn away in twilight,
The hawks are circling the western cliffs
Over the bones of hawks
That circled the western cliffs
Over the bones of hawks.

So imminent is knocking on the door
Or, without knocking,
The door slow opening,
Would they have listened
Had some voice tried to tell them:

City of mine, try to be beautiful!

Ever the longed-for light is rising
On the mountains, O my city,
Be patient, very patient,
There is time?

Some of the Boys a Little While Had Names

I speak of a street in Denver, Colorado:
Out of the distances of Summertime
Came teamsters under apricot parasols,
So high, so stately moving
On the great green beautiful elephant sprinkling wagons
Raking the dust with rainbow tines of spray;
You could smell a rainy push of cool and scuff
The thunderheads between your toes and wander
Over the cinnamon-silvertip Rocky Mountains,
Never returning.

There were autumns of jingle-bob cattle and swallowfork cattle
Sloping out Downing Street,
Horses in sunbonnets, golden balls on the hames
Of the horse-collars,
And some of the boys a little while had names
As you'd name a sulphur-saffron star Arcturus,
Or name a child Joe Gans or Agamemnon,
Or name a nick a moon in an agate marble,
Discrete, distinguishable from the moon in the sky
As long as some could still recall the meaning.
But now there are no cattle passing by,
The crack of a drover's whip, if there were one
To crack a whip, would be phenomenal;
The moon is silence lighted by the sun.

The boys strode up the lion ramps and down,
They panted and they boasted and they rested
Paler than lily-white Pollux, lily-white Castor,
Handlebars under the trees like dappled antlers
Pleaching the moods of maple to box-elder
Until the trees, insensible to names
Of vests and watch-chains, golden vegetables,

Respected lusts and temperate honesties,
Quit being trees: there was no pollarding
For higher growth and slowly they came down
By fractures of mild tempests and new times.

You could ride your bicycle out Downing Street
To the very end where you had to make a choice:
You could go the way the cattle had to go
Or hook to the West toward Riverside Cemetery
Where people had to go, or you could be
Impractical about alternatives,
You could change the street each evening at the summons
Of tomorrow's candlepower by wick, by sun.

Streets Due West

>·|·‹›··O··‹›·|·‹

The end of every street a hill,
The top of every hill a line
Too indistinct in blue and blue
For any to divine,
Were just as strange as any street
That ended in a gleaming sail,
Or any wall ten chariots wide,
Sung in a golden tale.

All streets end in morality
Of fables told in human span,
Where three score years and ten are roofs
And spires to measure man,
Save these that end in blue and blue,
In peak and peak and sky and sky,
At seven on an April night,
Immeasurably high.

Something Starting Over

You don't see buffalo skulls very much any more
On the Chugwater buttes or down the Cheyenne plains,
And when you roll at twilight over a draw,
With ages in your heart and hills in your eyes,
You can get about as much from a Model-T,
Stripped and forgotten in a sage arroyo,
As you can from asking the blue peaks over and over:
> "Will something old come back again tonight?
> Send something back to tell me what I want."

I do not know how long forever is,
But today is going to be long long ago,
There will be flint to find, and chariot wheels,
And silver saxophones the angels played,
So I ask myself if I can still remember
How a myth began this morning and how the people
Seemed hardly to know that something was starting over.

Oh, I get along all right with the old old times,
I've seen them sifting the ages in Nebraska
On Signal Butte at the head of Kiowa creek.
> (You can drink from the spring where old man Roubadeau
> Had his forge and anvil up in Cedar Valley,
> You can look back down the valley toward Scottsbluff
> And still see dust clouds on the Oregon trail.)
I entered the trench they cut through Signal Butte,
And I pulled a buffalo bone from the eight-foot layer,
And I watched the jasper shards and arrowheads
Bounce in the jigging screen through which fell dust
Of antelope and pieces of the world
Too small to have meaning to the sifters.

One of them said, when I held the bone in my hand:
        "This may turn out to be the oldest bison
In North America," and I could have added:
        "How strange, for this is one of the youngest hands
That ever squeezed a rubber bulb to show
How helium particles shoot through water vapor."
And the dry wind out of Wyoming might have whispered:
        "Today is going to be long long ago."

I know how it smells and feels to sift the ages,
But something is starting over and I say
It's just as beautiful to see the yucca
And cactus blossoms rising out of a Ford
In a sage arroyo on the Chugwater flats,
And pretend you see the carbon dioxide slipping
Into the poverty weed, and pretend you see
The root hairs of the buffalo grass beginning
To suck the vanadium steel of an axle to pieces,
An axle that took somebody somewhere,
To moving picture theaters and banks,
Over the ranges, over the cattle-guards,
Took people to dance-halls and cemeteries—
I like to think of them that way together:
Dance-halls and cemeteries, bodies beginning
To come together in dance-halls where the people
Seem hardly to know that hymns are beginning too;
There's a hymn in the jerk of the sand-hill crawl of the dancers,
And all the gods are shining in their eyes;
Then bodies separating and going alone
Into the tilting uphill cemeteries,
Under the mesas, under the rimrock shadows.

I can look at an axle in a sage arroyo,
And hear them whispering, the back-seat lovers,
The old myth-makers, starting something over.

Song for a Climber

With the blast of the peaks in my armpits,
My hands stretched to the sun,
It's a fierce way up and a strong day up,
And a high course to be run ...
A camp-bird's shadow whips my face,
The bird has reached a higher place,
Up ... on ... up.

The sky above is a burning plate,
The range below, a dappled grid,
Old gorgeousness of snow in blue,
'Neath which the world is hid,
This pine once combed the lightning's hair
And fell to be my lichened stair,
On ... up ... to where?

Where the man trail ends in flying mist,
Where the soul trail tracks up amethyst,
Where all is high and nothing higher,
Worlds below and skies of fire.

Song for Silverheels

(from ... *And Perhaps Happiness*)

Whereaway?
O whereaway?
Over yonder mountain,
Yonder evening star,
Willow, willow,
Willow river far,
O my love,
I go where e'r you are.

Stories of Three Summers

>–+–→–•–O–◆–+–◄

Colorado
1776 ★ 1876 ★ 1976

I. 1776

Two hundred years ago
In the dog days of that summer
     Of Life, Liberty and Pursuit of Happiness
Two friars scuffing golden rabbit-brush
For the glory of God
And the Holy King of Spain
Were goading their guides,
Their cattle, dreams and horses
Down the Dolores River
And over the Uncompaghre Mesa
Where Colorado was going to be.

    They needed guides to show them where to go
    As we do now.

The guides were Utes,
Young men and boys
Who knew the roads of rivers and old trees
Their fathers and their fathers
Had long traveled
Under the Goose-Going-Moon,
Under the Star-That-Never-Marches.

Admiring citron trees
And stalks of sarsaparilla,
Fray Silvestre Valez de Escalante
Smoked his cigars,
Stared at the constellations,
Knowing no more than a prong-horned antelope
Of how a leaden statue

Of King George the Third
Had been melted into bullets
In New York.

Nor did he know
He'd never reach
What he was yearning for ...
Those holy missions
Blessed by the vespers of the Western Sea
In far-off California.

> *We never know*
> *Until long afterward*
> *If even then.*

Francisco Atanasia Dominguez
Was sick with chills and fever
While Lord Cornwallis
Was prodding his red-coat musketeers
Toward Flatbush
But knew nothing of it.
Nor did he know
Foreshadowings of *Figaro*
Were lilting in the singing heart
Of Mozart.

> *We never know.*

II. 1876

Ten decades of manzanita berries
Come and go on the Uncompaghre Mesa
The Fathers Escalante and Dominguez
Fade into waters naming the arroyos.

In Colorado Territory
Statehood long denied
Can be denied no longer.

Sagacious gentlemen in Oddfellows Hall
Puff out their wastecoats
Prouder than pouter pigeons,
Hitch up the galluses of their pantaloons
And slap each other on the back
To end their endless bickerings
Over a Constitution

> *For Beautiful Colorado*
> *Most Glorious Jewel*
> *In the Diadem of States.*

Ladies in sunbonnets plant sweet peas
Under windy trellises of chickenwire.
Snowballs blossom,
Doves coo to their mates,
Taffeta girls and mandolin boys
Sing old sweet songs at twilight
On the jig-saw front piazza.

Sales are brisk for ladies' linen collars
And Mustang Liniment, the Foe of Pain,
Hand-hammered horseshoe nails
Are in abundance

> *And rosewood coffins.*

The sun comes up with a bang on the
Fourth of July!
Bells! Whistles!
Stove pokers beating dishpans!
Parades! Parades!
Proud horses nodding plumes!

> Miss Neoma Haggerty
> Is *The Spirit of Liberty.*

A shuffling boy of a Negro slave intrudes,
Parading down the steet alone

In a tattered old Prince Albert coat,
The clapper of his hand-bell clangs
The *lost-child* clang of the mining camps,
He chants
>   *Loss Chile!*
>   *Loss Chile!*
>   *Loss Chile!*

They reach the park,
They hear *Centennial Hymn*
By John Greenleaf Whittier of Haverhill,
They hear *Centennial*
A poem by Lawrence Greenleaf
Proprietor
Of the Toy-and-Stationery Store.

The poem starts
>   *O, day, aforetime, ominous*
>   *and heralded with fears*
Continues through
>   Two thousand
>   and eighty-one words
And ends
>   *Till Freedom with her halo-light*
>   *pervades the world at last.*

Tumult drowses down the morning star,
Trumpeters sleep late,
Husks of skyrockets
Tangle the tumbleweeds
And business of the grasshoppers
Goes on.

On August 1 Ulysses Simpson Grant
Takes pen in hand and signs a piece of paper.

Another State begins to be a State
And over the long blue echoings

Of plains against the ranges
Eagles fly,
Beavers build dams
And there is joy
In Growth
And Progress
And Prosperity.

III. 1976

Another hundred years ...

Trails of pack-mules fade into vapor trails
To Elsewhere,
Any Elsewhere anywhere.

Here to Las Vegas
In two martinis flat!
Caesar's Palace!
Under the undulations of the desert
Trundling megatons
Kill yucca moths and prairie dogs
And mice,
Caesar's Palace trembles

And rolls dice.

We elbow through an opiate shadowland.

The air is foul,
The seas are sour,
Trees of the forest disappear,
Why do we cringe back home from blundering wars?
Why are too many people here?

We grin and grimace into apathy.

There is no laughter,
No delight,

If there be sunrise
Sunrise will be night.

I go out Washington Street to Washington Park,
Old men are fishing by the lake,
I say hello and ask one pensioner
        "Why do we call this *Washington* Park?"
        "Because we always did ... "
And the old man drifts
Like the bobber on his bait
Way back to when "they let us kids
        go swimmin' in Wash Park Lake
        before it made you sick."

Platoons of children trot around the lake
With placards on their backs
                Jogging for Jesus
I ask one straggler if he'd like to hear
Me tell a story about George Washington,
        "Is that your dog's name?
        "Does he bite?"

My beagle has a water-fight with a sprinkler,
The lake is rippling up the undersilver
Leaves of cottonwood and I pretend
I see the Washington Monument
Splitting the heavens
Like a whetstoned obelisk.

I make a rhyme:

        The first stone came from Bunker Hill,
        The last stone came
        From the Emperor of Brazil ...

The phallic obelisk takes off like a rocket
In a blaze of hatchets and cherry trees
Plugging a Washington's Birthday sale

Of sure deodorants
Or your money back.

I who tell those stories of three summers
Must not let allegory blunt
My plain intention
To interweave old tales of Colorado
With deeds of far-off patriots long ago
We try to celebrate
By mere coincidence
Of dates on calendars

Like saying *Happy Birthday*
To ourselves
As we click a stop-watch on oblivion.

Off to the west
Where my elm tree used to be
Before the beetles killed it
I see the Rocky Mountains
Trying to shoulder up
Above the violet-ochre smog
Of Jefferson County.

Jeffco we call it.

Jeffco, I ask,
How often do you think of Thomas Jefferson
In morning times and evening times?

The smog is drifting my way,
I can taste it.

I turn my car on Adams Steet in Denver,
John Adams, do I hear your voice?
Yours, Abigail Adams,
Bride of a President,
Mother of a President?

I hear one sparrow chirp.

I make another turn at Franklin Street,
You, Benjamin Franklin?
You lewd outrageous fellow!
Would we put up with the likes of you today
Even in Washington?

Washington … Washington …
I repeat the word … what does it mean!

At home I drowse in honeysuckle shadows,
Our heroes, where have *they* gone?
Where have *we* been?
What are *we* heading to?

There ought to be some moral
To my chronicles,
I am too old to break with my belief
The world is getting better

Yet …
My garden wall is a lens through which I see
Tortures of war on every continent
And across the alley
Little Felicita before she became a nun
Jerking the legs off grasshoppers.

Eyes half closed
I watch a bumblebee in the honeysuckle
Buzzing the sandy dynasties of Egypt
From flower to flower,
I hear the warble of a rosy breasted finch
Over the wheezings of the snow-bound elephants
Of Hannibal,
I hear a squatting sorcerer in Denver
Talking shop with a con-man in Babylon.

Out of the time-slosh of the tides
We've learned to crawl
And race the stars so soon,
We can't remember who we were tomorrow,
We can't remember who it was
Back in those quaint old days
Who walked the moon.

Do I hear terror singing into laughter?
Do I hear torture gasping into love?
Dare I believe more dreams than I can prove?
We never never know until long after

If even then

For centuries are only flicks
Of dragonflies
Over the granite mountains.

Wood

There was a dark and awful wood
Where increments of death accrued
To every leaf and antlered head
Until it withered and was dead,
And lonely there I wandered
And wandered and wandered.

But once a myth-white moon shone there
And you were kneeling by a flower,
And it was practical and wise
For me to kneel and you to rise,
And me to rise and turn to go,
And you to turn and whisper *no*,
And seven wondrous stags that I
Could not believe walked slowly by.

The Dragon Master

He built his hut on a beetling cliff,
And far above the plain as if
The highest moon could hardly rise
Unto the level of his eyes;
His crags are dragons that tried to creep
From the prairie sea and went to sleep
With heads uphill and backs worn thin
By the whetted wind they burrowed in.

At twilight where he goes to sit,
Unerring incidences fit
In such a way that when the sun
Has capped the foothills, one by one,
They sink like distances of scales
On flat collapsing dragon tails,
And he stares at them absently,
Like old Aegeus, out to sea.

Dissimilar is he and odd
Enough to hold himself a god
O'er men who fear a dragon's head,
And throng on his dead tail instead;
He sees fat cities glow afar,
Of men who never scorned a star,
He's old and mad and stark … but then
He looks downhill at moons and men.

The Prairie Melts

The prairie melts into the throats of larks
And green like water green begins to flow
Into the pinto patches of the snow.

I'm here, I move my foot, I count the mountains:
I can make calculations of my being
Here in the spring again, feeling it, seeing ...

Three granite mountain ranges wore away
While I was coming here, that is the fourth
To shine in spring to sunlight from the north.

A mountain range ago the sea was here,
Now I am here, the falcons floating over,
Bluebirds swimming foredeeps of the blue,
Spindrift magpies black and splashing white,
The winged fins, the birds, the water green ...

Not ocean ever now but lilies here,
Sand lilies, yucca lilies water-petaled,
Lilies too delicate, only a little while,
Lilies like going away, like a far sound,
Lilies like wanting to be loved
And tapping with a stick,
An old man tapping
The world in springtime with a stick.

This buffalo grass? O, you who are not here,
What if I knock upon your tombs and say:
The grass is back! Why are you still away?

I know the myth for spring I used to know:
The Son of God was pinned to a wooden truss
But he lived again, His blood contiguous

To mine, His blood still ticking like a clock
Against the collar of my overcoat
That I have buttoned tight to warm my throat.

Who was His lover? That might keep Him nearer.
Whom did He love in springtime fingering
All fruit to come in any blossom white?
Cupping His hand for tips of nakedness
And whispering:

> *"You are the flowers, Beloved,*
You are the footstep in the darkness always,
You are the first beginning of forever,
The first fire, the wash of it, the light,
The sweetest plume of wind for a walled town"?

I light my pipe. A heavy gopher sags
Into her burrow scarfed with striping snow,
So quick, so slow, I hardly see her go.

Yonder, a barbed-wire fence, and I remember
Without intention how a wire can twist
A gopher hole until it burns the wrist ...

And there are wrists like mine that hang in trees,
And overcoats like mine to mulch the stubble,
And there are houses where the young men say
It would be different if the harbors and
The looms were ours ...
The end of women wailing for a ship.

But sundown changes day to yesterday:
The purple light withdraws from purple light,
The listing mountains close the lilies tight.

Above the blackness still one falcon burns,
So high, so pale, the palest star seems nearer,
One fleck of sun, one atom-floating mirror.

His shadow will not strike this world tonight:

There is a darker homing hollow bone
Of wings returning gives to wings unknown.

My tilted skull? My socket eyes? Are these
With chalk of steers apprenticed to the grass
When mountains wear away and falcons pass?

No answer is.
            No policy of rock
Or angel speaks.
                    Yet there could come a child
A long time hence at sundown to this prairie,
A child far-generated, lover to lover,
Lover to lover, lover to lover over ...
(O I can hear them coming, hear them speaking
Far as the pale arroyos of the moon.)

The child could walk this prairie where I stand,
Seeing the sundown spokes of purple turning,
The child could whisper to a falcon floating:
"I am not lost.
                They told me of this prairie:
This is the prairie where they used to come
To watch the lilies and to watch the falcons."

This Trail

We may have been coming up a misty spring,
A summer of long fire, some autumn when
Those mountains over there were first thrown up
To make a purple windrow, but we needn't
Talk of the breaking down of a skull or blossom,
Or whether the hair lives longer than the heart,
Or how improbable it always was
That we should ever walk this trail together.

This is no night for winding clocks. I love you.

The Train Butcher

I sit on the back platform of the train
Dragging my patent-leather buttoned shoes
Through embers of fireweed growing along the ties.
How slowly I go by! How long I use
The wonder of the mountains in my eyes
As if I were that very boy again.

There is a beautiful train butcher who comes
Still as a cat to the platform where I sit,
He props his basket on the hand-brake wheel,
He gives me grapes, he gives me chocolate,
He does not make me buy, he does not sell,
He gives me cornucopias of plums.

He's older than the hills and I am young,
He gives me colored eye-glasses through which
To see the whole wide world and all that's in it,
But I am rich with train whistles, I'm rich
With cinders falling half a dream a minute
On the sag of the rails the weight of the train has sprung.

The train butcher whispers under his cavernous coat:
Stop staring at the hills, no one will know!
Here are pictures of men and girls with no clothes on!
All yours! All yours! See what they're doing now!

All yours! These childish mountains now be gone!
All yours! No foolish woodlands in your throat!

All mine! And every cross-tie nudging *yes!*
All secret interlockings, all my own!
I finger the tongue of steel that snubs the brake
In the ratchet-wheel ... but a strange new train moves on,

Slides into satin valleys that awake
To naked music wilder than wilderness.

Far as tomorrow, this, and far ago,
The platform of the car, the hills, the smoke,
The smell of windrowed hay, the terrible shadow
Of the great train butcher's blue serge cowl and cloak,
Good and evil, Eden's ageless meadow,
A boy's new shoes the weeds go snatching through.

Gone is your train, my ancient, whistle and bell,
Gone are the rails, and I am come and gone
And gone and come through centuries I gauge
By crags the wings of butterflies grind down
A flick a season, so I say how sage
You were! How sage for teaching me so well!

Fine fellow, did you die in church or bed?
I miss you as I walk these rotted ties
Among the canyons of lost valley floors,
No tempter but the sunrise in my eyes;
Such grapes were yours, such sweets, such pretty whores,
And all love's wisdom that you left unsaid.

These Planks

>─┤◆>─●─<◆┤─<

These planks that were a town
Lie warping in the sun
As if a barrel tumbled down the peaks
Were shattered into staves.

You always wish these wasted towns were older,
It seems unreasonable for death to lack
Experience and do so well so quickly.

This Foreman

>─┼─◆>─O─<◆─┼─◄

"What did you see when girders rose?"
   "A house of steel, a net."
"What else?"
        "Men in their working clothes,
Men with their foreheads wet;
I saw them sway on the high steel beams,
But I knew their heads were wet."

"Did you see a workman slip and fall dead?"
   "I saw one leave the steel;
I heard what some of the others said,
And I saw the swallows wheel
Round the foreman with the twisted head,
Whose foot was half a heel."

"When the man fell, what did this foreman do?"
   "He sang, he sang like a swan
Of how two naked lovers loved
In a cage of steel till dawn;
He sang—and his mouth was a slit of dark—
Of a sword that could be drawn."

"You say you heard this foreman *sing?*"
   "I heard him sing like a swan."
"You say this foreman stopped to *sing*
When a man had fallen down?
(*He says he heard this foreman sing*
Like a swan when a man fell down.)"

"You heard this foreman testify?"
   "I heard each word he said."
"Now briefly what did the witness say?"
   "He said when the man fell dead,
He slid like a flash to the dead man's side
And gave the dead first aid."

"All right, now what did this foreman do?"
    "I heard him sing like a swan
About two naked lovers trapped
    In a web of steel till dawn."
"You swear to God you heard him *sing?*"
    "By God, that man's the one."

"Court please, I'll ask the witness more,
Court please, I wish to show,
Court please, the witness on the stand,
Court please, is trying to
Make light of what he saw and mock
The State, Court please, and you."
"Do you affirm that this foreman *sang?*"
    "I affirm that he's the one."

Now the bailiff hammers a terrible din,
But nobody shouts: Tin, tin, come in!
Because they all stare at the foreman instead,
Who licks the slit in his crooked head.

"You stayed there after twilight came?"
    "The twilight did not come;
The steel net shone like a russet flame
At the touch of the watchman's thumb;
The men went home and the watchman walked
His rounds slowly and dumb."

"All right, the twilight did not come;
You stayed, what happened then?"
    "I saw the foreman stealing back,
He climbed to the top again,
He moved in the misty girder net
 And he sang like many men."

"Court please, I'll ask the witness more:
What did this foreman sing?"
    "He sang the strength of steel and steel
In days past measuring;

He tapped the beams with a monkey wrench;
I could feel the high crane ring."

"You're sure it was a monkey wrench?"
    "He sang of a snare for love;
He called to the silver hounds of love
In the wooded moon above,
And I heard him cry 'The hounds are dead,
What am I dreaming of?'"

"Go on, you heard this foreman sing?"
    "I heard him sing like a ghost,
How a man gone down was a man to lead
The van of a falling host:
    'Let my green steel stiffen in the frost
To snare what men love most!'"

"What men love most? He sang of that?"
    "I did not understand,
For he sang of the living lives of men
As if the steel had spanned
Their lives with something true and cold
That nobody had planned."

"Did your family know that you were there?"
    "Your honor, I object!"
    "Sustained!"
    "That's all."
    "Go down the hall to the last door and collect
Your fee ... the last door on the right."
    "Poor chap, his mind is wrecked."

Two figures loitered down the hall,
And each signed for its fee.
    "I could not understand your song,
Explain the hounds to me."
    "Not here, fool! Climb the steel tonight,
The moon goes down at three!"

This Lake Is Mine

Spaniel and stick, I walk around a lake
In City Park in Denver, Colorado.
We walk an hour: an hour's an increment
Of history to any hickory stick,
Or town, or boy, or ghost, or lake of water.

This lake is mine: this popcorn gravel edge
Of water holding brass band overtures
And willow roots and carp and lilac roots,
And rumbling lightning thunderheads behind
The music-nudging rowboats and the swans;
And black behind the arc lights are the beasts,
The wolves, the stagnant bears, the city panthers,
But never a sound comes from the nodding bison
Dragging the gold-braid music through their beards.

There is a bell that calls the rowboats in
At evening's end and girls in organdy
And young men wearing flannel trousers come
To shore remembering the inland click
Of water in the willow-drooping places,
And lilac panther cries and far-off waltzes.

No other water ever smelled like this.
I was a little boy: I knew the feel
Of crisscross sleepy benches pinching green
And the blare of the beautiful beautiful big brass horns,
Then mother saying: "Come, we're going home ... "
Home was a black direction toward the beasts,
Home was a sleepy flavor in your mouth
Through cottonwoods to a yellow trolley car
With window sills that tasted of varnished varnish.

No other water ever was so still,
So still for grappling hooks engaging death.
Remember how she looked?

The broken garter?
The angled wrist? The dripping willow plume?
The high-laced patent-leather boots with tassels?
The amber-shining thigh?
                    It was a woman.
Women have legs but they are not like ours.

No other water ever was so quick
For making willow bark for knives to cut.
"What promise shall we keep, we've made so many?"
The willows walk away. They change their places.
"Which was our tree? I thought the tree was here."
"Of course I love you. Why do you keep asking?"

No other water ever was so slow
For making pines grow taller than a boy.

II

Now while I stroke these rushes with my stick
And chew this bitter twig of almond willow,
I see the blue bow of the Rocky Mountains
Bending around my city to the west,

Bending from Yucatan to arctic roses,
And spanning in one single summer's day
All seasons: springtime, summer, autumn, winter.

It's quiet here, but if I hook my wrist
At arm's length I can cover with my hand
The rattling steeples of the jagged rock
Slitting the cotton paunches of the hail.

Here it is lilac time, one kite still flying.
I follow the kite-string up the sagging sky
To crystal ranges where the pines as tall
As masts of ships are deep in summer snow,
Their tips a finger's length above the crust,
Like cotyledons in a glacial garden.
Against the violet ice I can discern

The spruces bristling on the lower hogbacks,
Like hairs of iron a horseshoe magnet drags
From little sand-pile mountains in a schoolyard.

So I go dreaming up a bellied kite-string
Into the old economies of water …
The dripping of the summer-inching glaciers,
The water trickling down this continent,
The water bringing beaver hunters back,
The water sluicing gold out of the mountains,
The water bloating oxen into gas,
The water changing cottonwoods to cities,
The water climbing lattices of clay
Into the root hairs of the grama grass.

The air is clear for seeing snow too far,
And I could tell the boy who flies the kite:
We are the lizards panting in the saltweed,
We are the gasping fish, the wilted larks,
The wetted finger hissing to the plowshare,
We are the dust that turns the sun to blue
Over the blistercress, the soda places;
And I could tell the boy who flies the kite
About the yellow cactus blooming here
Before this lake was here or we were here.

I lie upon my belly on the grass,
I whisper names of motorcars that glide
Reflected upside down among the fish …
De Soto, Hudson, Cadillac, La Salle,
The river men, the frosty men uphill,
I whisper names that are the names of ghosts …
Fitzpatrick, Lisa, Jedediah Smith,
Mackenzie, Coronado, Ogden, Hearne,
Singing the long song to the nameless mountains.

Where is the yellow gold, the fur, the amber?
Which is the river to the Seven Cities?

How far beyond the sunset are the mountains?
What mountain river flows into Cathay?

The snows have melted questions into answers,
The river singers slowly change to water:

Bill Ashley is a waterfall in Utah,
And Father Escalante is a river,
John Hoback is a river in Wyoming,
John Day's a river out in Oregon,
Kit Carson is a river in Nevada,
Bill Williams flows into the Colorado,
Jim Bridger is a lake that turns no wheel.

Some of the dead are water ...

        And my stick,

From walking far and changing histories
Of little things like ants on rainy flagstones,
Is blunted at the end.

       I whirl the stick.
I scar the lake, a sweeping shoulder stroke.
The drops of water splash into the gravel,
And there are lenses, if I needed them,
For altered history within one drop
Alive with lucid water animals
That perish on my shoe in sunlight warm
As sunlight sloping down the afternoon
The river namer, old Bill Williams, died,
Sunning himself, his back against a tree,
Somewhere in mountains no one knows about.
Maybe it helps, or ought to help, to think
Of microscopic water animals
And old Bill Williams drying in the sun,
As giving angel-like advice to us,
Telling us:

      Hurry! There is time to throw
Your stick into a high box-elder tree
To bring a winged samara spinning down!

Yet if you do not need a spinning seed,
Or only seed and not the spinning down,
You may have other uses for the time
It takes for not yet being dead …
                              Or loving.

III

The time it takes for not yet being dead
Is ticking in the watches in the pockets
Of people stopping cars beside this lake.
They come here to make love. They're not molested.
The motor runs a moment longer here
And stops as if it were not planned to stop.
It's not too dark to see a flying bird,
Yet dark enough for the wrist that turns the key
To turn the woods on on the other side.
They look like woods. Love tries to make them woods.

The lake is clouding as a mirror clouds.
There's naked silk against the gear-shift lever
And light comes from the wrong part of the sky
To make lips redder than the blood that burns
Into their upward-stroking syllables.

I snap my fingers and the lake is older,
The lids of eyes are older, and the lips;
The hairspring in a watch is measuring
The jerking in the muscles of a heart;
The grass is working and the trees are working,
The anther working and the needle pumping,
The heart is pumping and positions change:
A carp has crossed the shadow of a duck,
And deep within the dark mechanics of
A willow leaf tomorrow gropes for use.

Positions of the lovers change and change,
The knee, the wrist, the spine, the cheek, the thigh,
The eyes are open and the eyes are closed,

The muscles of the lips and tongues and throats
Make air make sounds: *I love you! I adore you!*

They hardly see the raindrops on the windshield,
They hardly see the evening on the fenders,
They hardly see a misty circling bird.

I know this bird that circles rainy water,
All silverness like dust of aspen bark:
Its name is Forster's tern, a random thing
Intent on fluttering in no direction;
But if I fix a sight-line from my stick
Across the water to some mountaintop,
The random bird will intersect the line,
Winging the very space he used before.
It may be fins that brings him back to fish,
I only know the circling bird returns.

The silver bird the lovers hardly see
And hardly need returns long afterward ...
Over the helix hairspring of the years,
Over the lake unfinished, love unfinished,
And I can hear a lonely whisper saying:

It must have been ... because I can remember
The way the water looked, and I remember
The mountains and the rain against the willow,
And I remember how a silver bird
Flew over us and over us and over us ...

So is there need for hills behind a face,
And wings against the transitory hills,
So would I take one cooling summer locust
Into my heart to sing beyond erosion;
And if I say this night to you, my lover:
        "The locusts are asleep," my heart is saying:
        "God bless you, but if Time outlive our God,
Time bless you, dear ... "
                        I whistle to my dog.

Time of Mountains

So long ago my father led me to
The dark impounded orders of this canyon,
I have confused these rocks and waters with
My life, but not unclearly, for I know
What will be here when I am here no more.

I've moved in the terrible cries of the prisoned water,
And prodigious stillness where the water folds
Its terrible muscles over and under each other.

When you've walked a long time on the floor of a river,
And up the steps and into the different rooms,
You know where the hills are going, you can feel them,
The far blue hills dissolving in luminous water,
The solvent mountains going home to the oceans.
Even when the river is low and clear,
And the waters are going to sleep in the upper swales,
You can feel the particles of the shining mountains
Moping against your ankles toward the sea.

Forever the mountains are coming down and I stalk
Against them, cutting the channel with my shins,
With the lurch of the stiff spray cracking over my thighs;
I feel the bones of my back bracing my body,
And I push uphill behind the vertebrate fish
That lie uphill with their bony brains uphill
Meeting and splitting the mountains coming down.

I push uphill behind the vertebrate fish
That scurry uphill, ages ahead of me.
I stop to rest but the order still keeps moving:
I mark how long it takes an aspen leaf
To float in sight, pass me, and go downstream;

I watch a willow dipping and springing back
Like something that must be a water-clock,
Measuring mine against the end of mountains.

But if I go before these mountains go,
I'm unbewildered by the time of mountains,
I, who have followed life up from the sea
Into a black incision in this planet,
Can bring an end to stone infinitives.
I have held rivers to my eyes like lenses,
And rearranged the mountains at my pleasure,
As one might change the apples in a bowl,
And I have walked a dim unearthly prairie
From which these peaks have not yet blown away.

To Anachronism

>─┼─◆>─◦─<◆─┼─<

We shall not be remembered. If we are,
Let there be hope in this: the world is new,
So new indeed that we may be confused
With men who feared a warlike god and who
In penitence built gray cathedral spires …
Confused within the myth-bright circle of
Bold kings who killed with quicker strokes than ours,
Such heroes as with high Achilles strove
Against a city and a city's gods.

We shall not be remembered. If we are,
Let time's dispersion of the year and hour
Join us to shepherd men who knew a star
Was holier than we who measure it,

But never hear it singing to its kind …
Men who raised altars to the sun and wind,

Who filled the shadows of the misty wood
With creatures made for love and nothing more;
Who, fearing more than we, were less afraid,
Though there were seas beyond which lay no shore.

We shall not be remembered. If we are,
The world is new, so new and so unused
To far remembering, take hope in this:
We and the elder dead may be confused.

To a Young Man Flying the Pacific

>-+-+>-+-O-+-<+-+-<

Reindeer herders watch you go,
Roaring shadow on the snow;
Jungle bird and coral flower
Hear you droning hour by hour.

There were reindeer in your book,
Borneo was in your book,
Burma was a name that meant
A golden cage in the animal tent.

Singapore was hard to spell,
China had a temple bell,
Oceans that you crayoned blue
Have come desperately true.

What meridians today
Are you crossing far away?
Arctic vapor, tropic mist
Ticking, ticking, on your wrist?

Here at home the suns go down
West of every eastern town,

West of every western place,
Sinking into ocean space ...

Sinking to rise up behind you,
Suns we've blessed and told to find you;
Fused with dawn, you blaze a path
Of thunder-doom and blinding wrath

For huddled shores where squinting eyes
Of folly must behold the rise
Of sun and sun and sun and sun
With agony for what was done.

Tomorrow Is Too Plausible

Tomorrow is too plausible forever
where the wind is,
where the sea is,
Yet can a man behold
beyond the trash-rack capsule of one planet
more than his epitaph a glacier cuts.

More beautiful,
an old man saying *Monday, Tuesday, Wednesday* ...
than all the burning of Aldebaran,
More mystical
than eel or bull or trellised vine or stream or grass
or hackled falcon plume,
an old man saying *Monday, Tuesday, Wednesday* ...

The finger wrinkling a bowl of cream a child's way
shall caliper the plunging of the worlds,
let all the glowworm suns go out forever,

let be the last tall town a scraping tool
clamped in the nudge of ice,
This shall be true:
the road was measured and the glory sung,

the wide seas ticking on a little dial,
all substances the syllables of primers,
and all meridians, the arctic white, the green,
within the palm as if a boy were shaking
shadows of a willow down his garden.

These towers?

These bright extractions fabricated over the whale-path
to the jutting rock?

These glassy elements all sluiced of cobble upward into
the shining thrust of gulls?

Is there a desert sill of any city seven-deep to influence
the prodding of the mole? *Go not that way! This was
their very passion and their beauty!*

The phosphor out of Hector is diffused: no atom knows
its name and Macedon is sifted in a screen as flakes of antelope and
teeth of men are sifted from the rim-rock of Nebraska.

The slitting steel that rivets earth to heaven?
How does it differ from the slow flint knife
when the sun goes down,
when the sunflower turns at evening to the east,
when the face begins to feel the separate weight of the cheek,
when nothing but yourself can tell you what you are?

How does the crackle of the hundred-and-seventh floor in your ear-
drum or the crackle in your eardrum of the under-river tube differ
from the crackle in your eardrum when you come to a mountain grave
at timberline and wonder who it was?

Strong and secure these tendrils of the steel
as prairie children swaying up the morning tumbleweed
for a school bus blowing a dusty trace the bison scarped ...

Strong as the whisper to a tenement wall:
Nevada, Mississippi, Oklahoma,
strong as the piñon song that ripples harbors,
strong as the voice the loom hears and the plowshare,
Ohio, Alabama, North Dakota,

Missouri, Colorado, Oregon ...

America!

America!
where a horse takes you,
where a ship takes you,
where they said it would always be like what you want
        it to be,
where they always said you could be what you have to be,
where they always said you could get another chance!

Build your tower so high so cold
you see your breath a summer noon,
set-back windows,
set-back thousand,
higher, higher, set-back thousand,
strong while they believe in Utah,
Carolina and no stronger,
Minnesota and no stronger.

Strong the tower as answering:
        The angels in my heart are not in yours!
        I hate you! You possess the things I lack!
        The blood in me is not the blood in you!
        Tomorrow is my power and your destruction!

Strong and secure the tower as wayfaring
beyond the starving plenitudes of wheat,
beyond the quarrel of the smith's apprentice,

Strong as the heart to meet the butcher men,
the throat to gag the rasping of the gas,
the strange electric hymns
calling the blowflies now
to battle quicklime for your jell of blood.

We rise,
we take direction
and we move
against the lapse and lag of distributions,
to learn by error
and to learn by error:
there is no peace implicit in the iron,
no wisdom in the agony to be wise,
no freedom in the frenzy to be free,

Save by some fortunate felicity,
all curious of earth and every brute,
all-transfusing stranger into kinsman,
and very simple as an old man saying
Monday, Tuesday, Wednesday in the evening,
And certain of the sunrise
as a man might say:

> *We will rise early,*
> *We will ted the hay.*

Trial by Time

Out of the old transgressions of the seas
We come,
Encroachments of the land,
No vestige of beginning,
No prospect of an end.

Salt of the blood is ocean bathing still
Each cell of brain and heart
Burning uphill.

Out of the tide-slime
Credulous we come,
Singing our latest God stabbed and perfumed,
Springing the eye of the enemy from the socket,
Building a ladder to a broken bird,
Meadow and mine to the pocket,
Dream to the word.

Out of the sluggard butcheries we come,
Cowering so at night in a white cold sweat,
Staring at hills and lovers,
Yet strange with a fairer courage,
To us of all beasts given,
To meet with flaking hair and nostril numb
The ice-long ice-long dream of peace on earth,
Somewhere on earth,
Or peace in heaven.

Two Rivers

Two rivers that were here before there was
A city here still come together: one
Is a mountain river flowing into the prairie;
One is a prairie river flowing toward
The mountains but feeling them and turning back
The way some of the people who came here did.

Most of the time these people hardly seemed
To realize they wanted to be remembered,
Because the mountains told them not to die.

I wasn't here, yet I remember them,
That first night long ago, those wagon people
Who pushed aside enough of the cottonwoods
To build our city where the blueness rested.

They were with me, they told me afterward,
When I stood on a splintered wooden viaduct
Before it changed to steel and I to man.
They told me while I stared down at the water:
If you will stay we will not go away.

Swallows

The prairie wind blew harder than it could,
Even the spines of cactus trembled back,
I crouched in an arroyo clamping my hands
On my eyes the sand was stinging yellow black.

In a break of the black I let my lashes part,
Looked overhead and saw I was not alone,
I could almost reach through the roar and almost touch
A treadmill of swallows almost holding their own.

Waltz Against the Mountains

We are waltzing now into the moonlit morning
Of a city swung against the inland darkness
Of the prairie and the mountains and those lights
That stab from green to red and red to green.

The music ends. We lean against the sill
Feeling the mountains blowing over us.

What keeps on moving if your body stops?

I ask you this as if we were not new,
As if our city were an ancient city.
I ask you this in Denver, Colorado,
With a moon for the year's end over your naked shoulder.

Denver is younger than a white-haired man
Remembering yellow gold up to the grass roots.
They tell of eagles older than Denver is:
I search the crystal edges of the twilight
For birds still floating over these prairies and
These mountains that had floated over these prairies
And these mountains when there was no city here.

I walk alone down Blake Street and Wazee,
Looking for asters growing through the hub
Of a wheel that brought my city up from the prairie;
But a welder's mask with purple eyes is hanging
From a peg in a wall where a yellow ox was tied
The night the people came in a wagon to rivet
The steel of a set-back tower to a set-back tower.

I was pulling hair from the trunk of a cottonwood tree
The longhorn cattle rubbed when a sudden man

Started tossing red-hot rivets up through the leaves,
Scorching the amber varnish of the leaves.
He made the red-hot rivets stick to the sky.
I had to quiet the glowing clatter down
The frozen silence of a long long time;
I had to leave the tree and look for another.

The prairie twinkles up the Rocky Mountains.
Feel how the city sweeps against the mountains;
Some of those higher lights, I think, are stars.
Feel how the houses crowd and crack uphill.
The headlands buckle with too many houses.
They're trying to find a place where they can stand
Until the red lights turn to green again.

I'm only half as old as the city is.
I'm younger than an old box-elder tree;
I'm hardly older than the old cathedrals,
Yet I remember primroses and yucca
Out there where all those houses are tonight.
We children gathered primroses and yucca,
We gathered sand lilies and cactus blossoms.

But there's hardly a child in all the sleeping children
From here to where we think the stars begin
Who sleeps in a room where a child, his father, slumbered.

When you wake in the morning tracing a drowsy maze
In the wall paper the sunrise trembles through,
The ceiling never whispers old directions
A ceiling learns from leading old men's eyes.
Off on that prairie frozen cattle flatten
With snow you cannot tell from moonlight on
Their shoulders and with darkness-clotted skulls
And darkness sagging in their hollow flanks;
And through those mountains black above this prairie
Are other animals alive and dead,

Some warmer than the rocks and some as cold,
And we are here, moving ourselves in music.

What keeps on moving if your body stops?

Mine is a city that has never known
A woman on a high wall looking down
Forever on the firelight of her kinsmen.
You're only a woman looking out of a window;
There are no ships, no smoking sacrifices,
And what we make, we are, and it is finished.

There's hardly time to speak beyond the flesh
In a city where the young men are always finding
A better place to start a cemetery.
Yet when this darkness cools the trembling tips
Of music in your breasts and earth has found
More certain use for me than waiting for
A woman on a wall, *what keeps on moving?*

We used to know, we don't know any more.
But I have seen enough of hills and blood,
And lovers and old men and windowsills,
The bones of churches and the bones of mountains
To know how far we may have come together,
And where we're going for a little way.

So late you came up to these mountains from
A valley by the sea you hardly know
Yet where to gather blossoms of wild plums;
But part of what you are was here before
You came, and part of what you were is gone.
Already melting snow moves through your shoulder,
Atoms of hills are warm within your shoulder,
And somewhere in your fingers that press my fingers
Are particles of corn the bison made
When their bodies clogged the river in the spring.

You are a woman younger than the city,
You are a woman older than the city,
You are the mountains changing into woman,
You are a woman changing into prairie.

See how the moon goes down behind those mountains.
The hills with every waning moon are lower.
They cannot last. They go where we are going.
They wear away to feed our lips with words.

The moon's a sand lily petal floating down
Behind the blue wall of the Rocky Mountains.
I see you as a woman on that wall,
Stepping down crumbled distances forever,
One terrace of a mountain at a time,
One terrace of a prairie at a time,
Until you join your kinsmen at the sea.

What keeps on moving while the mountains linger?

It may be something spoken at a window
About the uses of some hill we've borrowed,
Or something a welder sings to a cottonwood tree,
Or something the seasons make the lovers say
When it's summer on the plains and spring on the ranges,
And we follow weeks of lilacs up from the prairie
Into lost towns of the mountains and return
With lilacs when the hay is being cut.

Words for Leadville

By the brewery pond in California Gulch
A blind man taught me how to slit a trout
And gut it with my thumb.
                              A dead fish squeaks.
That I remember and the old man's thumb,
The thumbnail cracked with dynamite and granite;
A mountain had exploded in his eyes.

I smelled the spruces and the shadow of
Mount Massive on the brewery, and I saw
The lights of Leadville, and I passed my hand
Through drops of yellow water dripping from
A wooden flume into the yellow roses.

You can't get out, the mountains are so high,
You have to stay in Leadville till you die.

They called me in to supper: there were prayers,
And marmalade and venison and oysters —
        "We thank Thee, God, for these, Thy bounteous gifts"
And polished lamps and perfumed ladies rustling,
And gentle bearded men and bright nasturtiums,
And there was beer and trout and cheese and milk.

One day long afterward up here I asked
Four people where the brewery used to be.
They didn't know, but I found where it was:
Part of a fence was left and a briar rose.

It was a quiet Leadville Sunday morning:
The empty mountains, inside out, so still
You couldn't even hear the crackle of
The wooden props that tried to hold them up.
They looked like heaps of poked-up panther skins,
Stretching and sagging, yellow in the sun.

The city that had slid into the valley
Had settled in a pattern for an hour,
Most of the steeples pointing toward the sky.
The motorcars of tourists late to bed
Were white with frost wherever there was shadow,
But dripping where the sun struck the enamel.

The dusty tires were cool, you couldn't see
The stains of gentians nor the blood of chipmunks.
The whores were sleeping with their shades pulled down:
The tame coyote that one had in her window
Yawned when I tapped at him, as if a tap
From the outside of the window had no meaning.
A man who no one seemed to think was dead
Lay in the walk with flies about his lips;
I stepped across him as the others did,
All on their way uphill to the tolling churches.

It's uphill to the Wolftone mine,
It's uphill to the Matchless mine,
It's Sunday in the Terrible,
It's Sunday in the Chrysolite,
It's Sunday in the Waterloo.
The angels count the sparrow bones
In the Pittsburgh mine and the Printer Boy,
It's Sunday dripping in the Yak.
The angels count the sparrow bones
In the Mike and the Resurrection.

    "We thank Thee, God, for these, Thy bounteous gifts."

                ❊   ❊   ❊

I walk alone up Harrison Avenue
Remembering … remembering myself …

But I remember more than I remember:
The blood of time, the wincing of the earth,
The spasms of the ranges wrinkling down

Into the silver crucibles of lead,
Gold in the burnt rock, gold in the water sands,
Gold in the tangled roots of purple currants.
Wasn't I there then?
                    Something?
                                A timber thing
When August dried the velvet in the antlers
Of a thousand centuries?
                            When sloths were cool?
When lightning nicked the smell of ivory smoke
From April mastodons?
                        How slow the beasts
To crumble golden pathways through this quartz!
How slow the generations of the fish
Rubbing their autumn bellies on this gold,
Fish in the slurry choking floods of spring
Clogging their crimson gills with tumbling gold!

The gold lay still so many afternoons
So blue, so cold, so cold in summertime
The nutcrackers could see their cawing frozen,
And many elephants had turned to stone
And many fish to shale before the day
When Abe Lee hollered seven hundred miles:
        "By God! I've got all California
        Right here in this here pan … "
A goose quill full of gold!
A coffin full!
Acres of slopping gold!
Oceans of gold!

    "By God! My wife can be a lady now … "

Opera houses slopping down the flumes!
Whisky slopping over the riffle blocks!
Railroads! Moonlight! Diamond-studded garters!
Necks for nooses! Smelters! Homes for orphans!
Gold for a snowshoe priest and a quart of milk!

For colleges! For jigsaw senators!
Surgeons! Orchids! Bells for monasteries!
Mirrors for the ceilings of the brothels!

> "Now by the golden mirrors in this room
> Your flesh can love me more than you can love me ... "

Moonlight sliding over the riffle blocks!
Warm pneumonia over the riffle blocks!
Blood on the sawdust floor and a whisky cry:

> "We'll all go back and join Abe Lincoln's army!"

And seven hundred miles away the brides
Are chanting on the banks of the Missouri:
> "When shall we come?"
>   "Come when the grass begins!"

                    ❊   ❊   ❊

Deep in the rocky pages of the hills
Like bookmarks, lilies of the sea are printed.
A sleepy woodchuck winters in the earth,
Nosing his way through lilies petrified
And seams of country rock and porphyry ...
He curls against a frozen tide of *silver!*
Bonanza silver!
> *Silver!*
> *Silver bullion!*

The carbonates are clanging like a bell!
The mountains ring, the mountains swing!
The clappers of the mountains crack!
The silver cracks
And the single jacks
And the hammers bang,
And the hair grows long
And the ear is thatched
To hold a match as dry as bone
To light a fuse to crack the stone!

The whipsaw buckles in the pitch,
The bright axe chops and slits and chops,
The wood tick stops and runs and stops,
The log chain hooks a jangled hitch.
They tug at logs, the roaring men,
The frightened men, the coughing men;
The sweating salt is caking on
The tenderness behind their knees,
Sweating resin oozes noon
Out of the wounded trees.

With midnight whisky in their skulls
They drag the bloodshot forest down,
The mortise, chip and spike and lock
The forest underneath the town,
The giant powder nausea roars
Through rooms and tombs with silver floors.

Fifteen acres rib a mine,
Yellow gold to the Yellow pine,
Silver spruce to the silver ore,
The bristlecone shall drip no more
The long rain down its needles.

Logs to rib the Congo Mine,
Logs to rib the Yellowjacket,
Logs to rib the Dunderburg,
The Dome, the Law, the Iron, the Hope,
The sallow joinery of lungs ...
        "Oh Christ! I want to get out of here!"
Smuggler, Oro, Little Eva,
Yankee Doodle ...
                Gone Abroad!

Logs for a stamp mill tom-tom all night long,
Tom-tom drums for a can-can dancer's grunt,
Can-can drums for a tin-horn gambler's clink:
        "I'll bet my moccasins!"

"I'll bet my squaw!"
"My pick, my candle butts, my fuse, my pork!"
"I'll bet a dollar!"
"Fifty thousand dollars!"
"By God! I'll bet my banks!"
"I'll bet my smelters!"

                    ❖   ❖   ❖

Horn silver?
            Blossom rock to flower again?
Their fingers tweak the last wick into smoke.
The dancers flicker down.
                    The cut-glass planets
Have tightened Tiger Alley into frost,
And Stillborn Alley squeaks like rats that squeak
Against the starry fetus on the dump ...

    No larkspur for you, child, no gates to open,
    Never to live and love until it hurts,
    Never returning, never being sleepy ...

The miners go to sleep remembering
The hog kettles of home. They go to sleep
On beds of juniper remembering
The nests of wasps that hang from far-off ridgepoles,
A well sweep and a face and a mullein stalk,
The smell of hay-juice caking on a scythe,
Remembering preachers and the thighs of women.

The miners sleep so deep they do not wake;
The miners change to angels playing harps,
They sing along the golden streets of heaven.
The stakes they drove into the crusted snow
To claim the bitter nodules of the flint
Are washed away. The shining foil is gone.
The earth so sour behind the cabin door
Is sweet with raspberries and sweet with roses.
The old squaws chatter up the long blue trails,
They change to ghosts that rattle plum-stone dice.

The lobes of glaciers melt. The deep mines fill
With water inching upward black and still,
The cobwebs bind the windlass at the top,
The plumb-line spiders dangle till they drop.

I stroke, my palm across the frozen slag.
What latch to lift?
                  What step to take uphill?
The ranges fold the hay into their blueness,
The blossoms drip with night, the planets rise
Into the ordered schedule of my hunger
For what has been, continues, and will be.

Yet this I tell you. This is practical
Against whatever custom in your heart
There is for shaping ruins into thresholds:

Here is a town with houses tenanted,
Here is a town with silent houses crumbling,
If you are overtaken, they are shelter,
If you are cold, their splinters will make fire,
If you are rich, there will be purple asters,
If you are poor, there will be purple asters,
And if you are resourceful you can file
A silver dollar to a cutting edge,
And cut, not one, but any hundred asters,
Saying:
        "I cut a hundred purple asters,
          Using a knife I made out of a dollar!"
And if you have a watch, your watch will tick,
And you can count the beatings of your heart,
While roots of ferns are splitting particles
Of time from granite and the corpuscles
Of blood within you alter their confusion
A tombward instant irrevocably.

FERRIL'S SENSE OF PLACE

Thomas J. Noel

>─┤◆>─O─<◆┤─<

The Rocky Mountains have inspired forests of bad poetry. As the British wit, playwright, and critic Oscar Wilde noted after a visit to Colorado, the Rockies just seemed too high for poets to climb. Those magnificent mountains left most writers groping for words.

Thomas Hornsby Ferril also cringed at what he called the "God-finding" poetry and the "low-grade mysticism" of most verse about the Rockies. Undeterred by the gush of rhymesters, the Denver poet wrestled for most of his life with the mountains. He knew them too well to be sentimental and sloppy.

Nor did Ferril share the alienation, anger, and negativism of some modern poets. His poetry was generally a positive analysis, even a celebration of western history and landscape. Peter Viereck, asked by the Library of Congress to survey modern American poets during the 1950s, concluded:

> Ferril, at his best, has an enchantingly beautiful sense of wonder which is closer to the best French surrealists than to the star-spangled, 200 percent American, pseudo-folklore of his regionalist culture-hounds and adoring club women. ... If a thousand geniuses of the art of poison-pen united to invent the perfect Kiss of Death for a good poet, they could think of nothing grimmer than 'the poet laureate of the Rocky Mountains.'

For better or worse, Ferril was the unofficial poet laureate of the Rockies and the official poet laureate of Colorado. But he did not let the mountains overwhelm people; he used them as a backdrop for the human drama. "Magenta," for instance, begins with an exquisite description of the mountains around Central City and then evolves into an insightful look at the role of women in mining camps. Likewise, his urban poems tell a story as well as describing a setting. "This House in Denver," for example, is not just a description of old Denver but a prayer for historic preservation.

Born in a gold rush and raised on subsequent mineral booms, Denver was built fast and recklessly. Each generation seemed hell-bent on tearing down the edifices of preceding generations to erect its own monuments—be they parking lots or acrobatic towers of glass and steel and concrete. The new downtown towers—human filing cabinets—climbed skyward to measure egos and greed.

Ferril, like the pioneer generation of Coloradoans he chronicled, worried about Denver's fate. He not only criticized thoughtless demolitions, he became a Denver Landmark Preservation Commissioner in 1973, seven years after the commission was created, to identify and protect buildings of historical, architectural, and geographical significance. On the commission Ferril took aim at the barbarian newcomers who were ransacking his city. With magic landmark plaques he and his colleagues warded off the demon disguised as renewal.

This poet followed a cardinal rule of good writing: write about what you know. Ferril wrote about the places and people he knew in hundreds of poems published in local newspapers and in national journals such as *The New Yorker* and *Harper's*. Who knows how many unpublished poems he wrote? A friend's illness, a building's demolition, almost any occasion might inspire Ferril to write a poem or to respond to pleas and would pen a eulogy or reflection.

Nothing was too prosaic to capture the poet's attention. He wrote "Sidewalks in Denver," published exclusively in *This Week in Denver*, June 21–27, 1982:

My sidewalk out in front
is made of flagstone
scuffed by feet like mine
and chipped by frost
into shapes of continents,
oceans and islands.

You see them best
on a rainy April day.

I give them names.
I sail my ship
through the Straits of Marigold
past Lilac Harbor
up to Punkin Peak
where I mull a thousand years or so
on the mixed-up world below. ...

Life was poetry and poetry was life for Tom, as he insisted on being called in person while using the formal Thomas Hornsby Ferril in print. He measured life with poetry, claiming that "poetry is as accurate as mathematics, yet goes further. ... Poetry, is a lazy shortcut to more experience than you can get anywhere else."

"Always Begin Where You Are," Ferril entitled one poem. That title was the essence of his work, reflecting his firm sense of place. Ferril's life began—and ended—at Ferril House, designated a historic landmark by the city of Denver and a literary landmark by the American Library Association.

Ferril House sits at 2123 Downing Street on the edge of Five Points, one of Denver's oldest and poorest neighborhoods. Yet many fine Victorian houses of the 1880s have inspired recent regentrification of what was originally a middle-class neighborhood within walking distance of downtown.

Tom Ferril's great aunt and uncle, John and Joanna Palmer, built the house in 1889. In 1900 Joanna's niece, Alice Ferril, her husband Will, and their three young children joined the Palmers in the house. Twenty-one years later, Will and Alice's son Thomas married and brought his wife Helen to live in the house along with his parents and relatives. Tom and Helen's only child, Anne, was born there in 1922. Tom Ferril, the last family member to live in the residence, died there on October 28, 1988.

The two-and-a-half-story, red-brick dwelling is a typically eclectic Victorian wherein Ferril wrote far from typical poetry. Crowded onto an old-time Denver lot measuring 25 by 125 feet, Ferril House is an anachronism. Its Victorian rooms were filled with books from Ferril's father, Will C. Ferril. Will was a biblioholic, as well as a journalist, secretary of the Colorado Historical Society, and author of a still useful who's who of prominent white, male Coloradans entitled *Sketches of Colorado* (Denver: The Western Press Bureau, 1911). He collected some three thousand books and toward the end of his life inscribed each book "Thomas Hornsby Ferril from Will C. Ferril."

Like many houses, Ferril House was altered over the years to accommodate the changing needs of its residents. Artist Anne Ferril Folsom reminisced in 1996:

> Closing down that house after my father died in 1988 was not easy.
> Five generations of Ferrils, including my own daughter Cameron,
> had lived there. It was a dear family to grow up in, but it wasn't all
> moonlight and roses living with a working poet. Father wrote in
> his third-story studio next to my bedroom. Many a night I fell
> asleep while he was still writing. I'm still dazzled by his poetry, by his
> ability to create sharp, illuminating images that nobody ever saw
> before.

In 1996 the house was reincarnated as the Colorado Center for the Book, part of a national organization that promotes literacy and reading. The center sponsors Denver's annual Rocky Mountain Book Festival and Ferril Poetry Prize, and welcomes the use of Ferril House for literary events and poetry readings.

Ferril spent 42 years of his life as the publicity manager at the Great Western Sugar Company Building in lower downtown Denver. For three decades from around 1932 to 1968 Ferril edited two company magazines, *Through the Leaves* and *The Sugar Press*, for which he was the writer, editor, designer, and photographer. The unsigned articles are mostly technical pieces on topics such as growing techniques, fertilizers, moisture, soil balance, and crop rotation. His job at the Great Western Sugar Company, once Colorado's largest agricultural outfit, allowed Ferril to rub shoulders with executives, sugar plant employees, farmers, and field workers. In his press releases and company articles, Ferril provided encouragement, advice, and congratulations to the many sugar beet farmers and farm communities dealing with Great Western. He also produced movies showing how to better cultivate these big ugly beets. In *The Rocky Mountain Herald*, September 25, 1960, Ferril wrote about his life at the office:

> There's plenty of work to do—a farm magazine to get out and news stories and photographs. The sugar beet harvest is about to begin. Starting of the campaign always makes me feel like an old firehorse. I like the hum and smell of the factories, the roar of the beets tumbling from the scales into the slicers, the lingo of the farmers and factory men. ...

Although the Great Western Sugar Company is no longer in operation, the Sugar Building survives as a National Register Landmark in Denver's Lower Downtown Historic District. This neoclassical structure was built in two stages as the company grew. Architects Aaron Gove and Thomas Walsh, who designed many nearby warehouses and Union Station, were responsible for the original four-story structure as well as the two stories added in 1912. This grey brick gem is now ghostly, boarded up, and empty. The interior retains its original antique bird cage elevator ridden by the ghost of Tom Ferril.

The Cactus Club, at 1621 Blake Street, is a 1990 building that Ferril never saw. It was designed to resemble three previous, demolished clubhouses of this literary luncheon club founded in 1911. Ferril became a member in 1920 and, as the longtime club secretary, handled correspondence and also wrote skits, light verse, and helped develop offbeat rituals for the self-styled "prickly eccentrics" who now comprise Denver's last all-male club. On the clubhouse walls are Ferril's ode to the Cactus Club, "Into This Hall," and several photographs of Ferril, including one of him and other Cacti standing around an outhouse in the dark of a winter night, grinning.

They have just unofficially installed the outhouse in front of Colorado's gold-domed capitol, whose rotunda murals are captioned with Ferril's poem, "Here Is a Land Where Life Is Written in Water." The outhouse was put behind the log cabin, which supposedly served as territorial capitol during the 1860s in Colorado City. It was moved to Civic Center for the 1959 Centennial celebration of the 1859 Colorado Gold Rush. In this and many other practical jokes and stunts, Ferril took glee. For this occasion he hastily penned a poem:

> ... as the rosy fingered
> Dawn
> Comes up across our
> Capitol lawn —

Let's all arise
Salute a man
Who gave our
First statehouse
A can!

A little house
Where we may heed
Some isolation from
The day
And gently pass
Our cares away. ...

Ferril also belonged to the Denver Posse of Westerners and the Mile High Club. At the far less respectable and now defunct Evil Companions Club, he held the office of chaplain. Now reformed or in their graves, this informal collection of bon vivants was organized in 1957 primarily by journalists. The club expired after its headquarters, the Auditorium Hotel bar, vanished in a blaze that some said was punishment from heaven. At any rate, the bar never reopened and the Auditorium Hotel was torn down for another parking lot. It was one of many demolitions that Ferril would contemplate in his poetry, as in this passage from the poem "Invitation," from *Anvil of Roses:*

Thundering tumbrels haul away
The sticks and stones of living cities,
In their place high tombstones rise
Higher than the poisons in the sky.

The only surviving clubhouse that Ferril frequented is the Denver Press Club, located at 1330 Glenarm Place in downtown Denver. A 1925 design by Ferril's friend and Colorado's most notable twentieth-century architect, Burnham Hoyt, the red brick clubhouse is trimmed in white terra cotta quoins and window surrounds that hint at the collegiate gothic mode.

The "Thomas Hornsby Ferril Memorial Pool Table" in the Press Club's basement commemorates his legendary, subterranean conquests. Upstairs the back corner dining table has a bronze inscription, "Thomas Hornsby Ferril Memorial Table" with a quote from the poet: "Dare I believe more dreams than I can prove." There is no question mark, leaving little doubt that Ferril dared to do a lot. On the wall, the rogues' gallery includes Paul Conrad's drawing of Ferril.

By writing so well about western places, Ferril assured his own place as the best poet the Rocky Mountains have yet produced. His poetry blesses the few old timers and many newcomers of the still raw and young Rocky Mountain region with a sorely needed sense of place.

Selected Prose

BLESS THE ABSENT TOURISTS

$\succ\!\!-\!\!\leftrightarrow\!\cdot\!\bigcirc\!\cdot\!\leftrightarrow\!-\!\prec$

P rospect of the worst tourist season Colorado has ever known should delight all civilized people. This is one of the minor compensations of the tire shortage. Tourists always should have been rationed anyhow. There aren't more than a hundred choice spirits east of the Mississippi who deserve to come to Colorado any year. We feel sorry for them but—*c'est la guerre!* As for the rest, let them stew in their own Corn Belt.

The mountain roads are getting pocked with chuckholes. I've been over a few lately. Each thump is a caress. May they never be repaired! Most of them should never have been built at all. Their only function was to enable people going nowhere to get there quicker. Those aimless bumper-to-bumper processions over Lookout and down Bear Creek, flavoring the dusty spruces with carbon monoxide, characterized the most futile period of our culture. The jolting of Grandma's sacroiliac, the spewing of the carsick babes, the back-seat jangling, the inter-car cursing, were the total accomplishment.

The economic plight of migratory poverty obscured the spiritual plight of migratory affluence. The rich from Oklahoma and Texas were as dismal as the poor. The Okies and Arkies had to practice a little Thoreau at every camp site; they had to put up with what they had; there were gypsy compensations of foraging; and a long dream of getting somewhere. The non-poor simply used their installment-bought cars to prove that Emerson was right when he said that the traveler brought back only what he took with him—his miserable noncurious self. You got somewhere as quickly as possible for the sole reason of getting back as quickly as possible: you didn't know loco from thermopsis, a magpie from a camp bird. You didn't have time—or brains to take time.

The ghost towns will be ghost towns again. Just how the ghost town chambers of commerce will handle this dilemma of inadvertently telling the truth about themselves is indeed tearful. A ghost town was always a problem. Its sole claim for immortality depended on playing dead. How to lure in a thousand tourists a day and maintain the necropolitan gloom was none too simple. There had to be comfort stations and cottage camps from which a multitude of devout intruders could peer at the last survivor. It was all so authentic you just had to buy a house and lot—so you bought up a tattered, jigsaw American-Gothic shack, gave it a dose of Frank Lloyd Wright, screens, a gleaming paint job, and built a garage. Pearl Harbor ended the Central City-Black Hawk real estate renaissance none too soon. Another year would have seen Cape Coddages shining all the way to Nevadaville, with Denver's picturesque fisherfolk spreading nets and lobster pots on the mine dumps.

It's all for the best. I do have sentimental pangs, however, about tearing up the old C. & S. narrow gauge to Leadville and Gilpin County. Some of this scrap may catch up with Colorado boys now touring the Orient. But when this mess is over, our ideas of roads, transportation and motorcars will be different. The long cross-country tours you used to take, and even relatively short intercity jaunts, will be by safe cheap air travel. Our late fanaticism for roads will give way to fanaticism for airports. In the change-over period you'll fly to Leadville in a revised bomber, then climb Mount Massive just for the hell of it in a jeep-train following some burro trail of the fifty-niners. You'll look down with Pisgah wisdom on aspens reclaiming many of the highways which never should have been built. It will be a pleasant sight. Colorado Springs will slowly convalesce from that horrible scar tissue of roads mutilating Cheyenne Mountain. Meanwhile let it stand as a testimonial to municipal stupidity.

—T. H. F., June 16, 1942

THE LANGUAGE OF SCIENCE

cientific authors have to be impetuous and exhibitionistic. Their books are frail as orchids. Scientific books must sell like hot cakes or die on the vine. This is because science moves too fast for books to keep up with it. Every morning you see a bleary-eyed bunch of scientists crowding into the public library to find out which of their colleagues on the graveyard shift has scooped them overnight at their own game.

There's never any hurry about poetry because the language of poetry is stable. The language of science, on the other hand, is the most unstable in the world. Last week you had a simple scientific word, say, *bunny*. Just nice little *bunny*. On Monday comes a flash from Johns-Hopkins that the right name is really *sulfabunny*. Tuesday Toronto changes the word to *sulfathiabunny*. On Wednesday the *Lancet* of London announces *sulphathiadesoxybunny* and on Thursday Philadelphia counters with *sulphathiadesoxyphederindrexellbiddlebunny*. On Friday all the printers go nuts and walk out saying to hell with it. So by next Monday the whole concept starts over with *Bun*.

—T. H. F., March 4, 1944

FREUD AND FOOTBALL

﹥━┥◆﹥━◯━﹤◆┝━﹤

As I look back over the intellectual caprices of the past quarter
century, I am amazed that the Freudians never took out after
football.

Let me set down, in nostalgic summary, some of the find-
ings that might have been made, had the Freudians not been sulking in
their tents.

Obviously, football is a syndrome of religious rites symbolizing the
struggle to preserve the egg of life through the rigors of impending
winter. The rites begin at the autumn equinox and culminate on the
first day of the New Year with great festivals identified with bowls of
plenty; the festivals are associated with flowers such as roses, fruits
such as oranges, farm crops such as cotton, and even sun-worship and
appeasement of great reptiles such as alligators.

In these rites the egg of life is symbolized by what is called "the
oval," an inflated bladder covered with hog skin. The convention of
"the oval" is repeated in the architectural oval-shaped design of the
vast outdoor churches in which the services are held every sabbath in
every town and city, also every Sunday in the greater centers of popu-
lation where an advanced priesthood performs. These enormous
roofless churches dominate every college campus; no other edifice com-
pares in size with them, and they bear witness to the high spiritual
development of the culture that produced them.

Literally millions of worshipers attend the sabbath services in these
enormous open-air churches. Subconsciously, these hordes of worship-
ers are seeking an outlet from sex-frustration in anticipation of violent
masochism and sadism about to be enacted by a highly trained priest-
hood of young men. Football obviously arises out of the Oedipus
complex. Love of mother dominates the entire ritual. The churches,
without exception, are dedicated to Alma Mater, Dear Mother. (Notre
Dame and football are synonymous.)

The rites are performed on a rectangular area of green grass orien-
tated to the four directions. The grass, symbolizing summer, is striped
with ominous white lines representing the knifing snows of winter.
The white stripes are repeated in the ceremonial costumes of the four
whistling monitors who control the services through a time period di-

vided into four quarters, symbolizing the four seasons.

The ceremony begins with colorful processions of musicians and semi-nude virgins who move in and out of ritualized patterns. This excites the thousands of worshipers to rise from their seats, shout frenzied poetry in unison and chant ecstatic anthems through which runs the Oedipus theme of willingness to die for love of Mother.

The actual rites, performed by 22 young priests of perfect physique, might appear to the uninitiated as a chaotic conflict concerned only with hurting the oval by kicking it then endeavoring to rescue and protect the egg.

However, the procedure is highly stylized. On each side there are eleven young men wearing colorful and protective costumes. The group in so-called "possession" of the oval first arrange themselves in an egg-shaped "huddle," as it is called, for a moment of prayerful meditation and whispering of secret numbers to each other.

Then they rearrange themselves with relation to the position of the egg. In a typical "formation" there are seven priests "on the line," seven being a mystical number associated not, as Jung purists might contend, with the "seven last words" but actually, with sublimation of the "seven deadly sins" into "the seven cardinal principles of education."

The central priest crouches over the egg, protecting it with his hands while over his back quarters hovers the "quarterback." The transposition of "back quarters" to "quarterback" is easily explained by the Adler school. To the layman the curious posture assumed by the "quarterback," as he hovers over the central priest, immediately suggests the Cretan origins of Mycenaean animal art, but this popular view is untenable. Actually, of course, the "quarterback" symbolizes the libido, combining two instincts, namely (a) Eros, which strives for even closer union and (b) the instinct for destruction of anything which lies in the path of Eros. Moreover, the "pleasure-pain" excitement of the hysterical worshipers focuses entirely on the actions of the libido-quarterback. Behind him are three priests representing the male triad.

At a given signal, the egg is passed by sleight-of-hand to one of the members of the triad who endeavors to move it by bodily force across the white lines of winter. This procedure, up and down the enclosure, continues through the four quarters of the ritual.

At the end of the second quarter, implying the summer solstice, the processions of musicians and semi-nude virgins are resumed. After forming themselves into pictograms, representing alphabetical and animal fetishes, the virgins perform a most curious rite requiring far more dexterity than the earlier phallic Maypole rituals from which it seems to be derived. Each of the virgins carries a wand of shining metal which she spins on her fingertips, tosses playfully into the air and with which she interweaves her body in most intricate gyrations.

The virgins perform another important function throughout the entire service. This concerns the mystical rite of "conversion" following success of one of the young priests in carrying the oval across the last white line of winter. As the moment of "conversion" approaches, the virgins kneel at the edge of the grass, bury their faces in the earth, then raise their arms to heaven in supplication, praying that "the uprights will be split." "Conversion" is indeed a dedicated ceremony.

Freud and Breuer in 1895 ("Studien über Hysteria") described "conversion" as hysterical symptoms originating through the energy of a mental process being withheld from conscious influence, and this precisely accounts for the behavior of the virgins in the football services.

The foregoing, I confess, scarcely scratches the surface. Space does not permit interpretation of football as related to dreams, or discussion of the great subconscious reservoirs of thwarted American energy that weekly seek expression through vicarious enjoyment of ritualized violence and infliction of pain. To relate football to the Oedipus complex alone would require, as it well deserves, years of patient research by scholarly men such as we find in the Ford Foundation.

I only regret that these studies were not undertaken a quarter century ago, when the Freudians were in full flower. It's just another instance, so characteristic of our culture, of too little and too late.

—T. H. F., September 10, 1955

ON THE OREGON TRAIL

⋙—⋘—◦—⋙—⋘

If there's anything more beautiful than approaching the North Platte Valley at sundown, I don't know what it is. Last week I had a few chores to do at Brush, Fort Morgan and Sterling in the South Platte Valley of Colorado, then dropped over to the Lodgepole Valley late in the afternoon and it was almost dark when I reached the North Platte Valley of Nebraska. Twice I stopped the car just to stare at the colors behind Courthouse Rock. It was as if some crazy Navajo had woven a blanket of light. I can understand how the forty-niners felt when they reached that valley—Courthouse Rock, Chimney Rock, Castle Rock, Table Rock, Scott's Bluff, Signal Butte and the rest—and on up the river to Fort Laramie and points west. As you circle back to Denver from the west end of the valley, the 84-mile stretch from Torrington to Cheyenne is as lonely a passage of western landscape as I know.

I never get to that part of the country without asking myself again and again the old puzzling questions about landscape. When I stop to stare at Courthouse Rock cut out of cardboard against a rainbow sunset, is the experience complete in itself? Or am I adding all I know from Washington Irving, from Parkman, from Mari Sandoz, from what I know of the millions who went that way including many members of my own family? If I were to drive my car just around the edge of Courthouse Rock would I see the campfires of the Sioux or the Minatarees?

Unquestionably the implications of history add much, perhaps everything. As Keats put it, the greensward means nothing until it has felt "the tread of a nervous English foot." I don't know that there's any point in being critical about landscape, but if you go in for it, avoid the spectacular. What you are trying to answer in the Alps or Himalayas is set forth on much simpler terms in the North Platte Valley of Nebraska. Signal Butte works as well as Everest. Nuances of prairie bring you quicker to the essence of the problem than chaotic peaks in stormy disorder.

One thing I'm always wishing in such exciting places is that the people who live there realize constantly how beautiful it is to be there at all. You wind down a hill into Sidney, Nebraska, on the Lodgepole.

It's all trees, a sort of poster town with the Lincoln Highway behind it. Some child has stuck a panting Union Pacific train across the main street to see how it looked. Do the insiders see what the outsider sees? I thought of Tom Wolfe and Robert Frost. One afternoon I was taking Tom Wolfe through Longmont, Colorado. The top was down and Tom stood up in the back of the car. He was fifteen feet high and with that lisping, stuttering, bellowing voice of his he said: "God what a wonderful place to live in!" And I asked him: "Do the people who live here know it?" The same question came up with Frost, driving one night to Boulder. We passed a too beautiful farm in the cottonwoods. There were lights in the windows. I've forgotten just how Frost put it because he's always coppering every premise four ways, but the force of his remark was that if the people were looking out at all, they were probably envying us on the highroad—going somewhere they couldn't go.

What it all comes down to is making something out of what we are where we are. Our most terrifying international problems are, at the core, provincial problems. Whether you're in Shanghai or Nuremburg, your horizon is neither nearer nor farther than it would be in Sidney, Nebraska. The service flags in the windows on the banks of the Lodgepole are only emblems of mankind dislocated and relocated through the inability of men everywhere on earth to make a local go of it anywhere. Local frustration generates the plundering nomad in us.

—T. H. F., November 3, 1945

The following is a condensed version of an interview with Thomas Hornsby Ferril by Tom Auer, from the article, "Probing the Art of Poetry," in the May/June 1981 issue of *The Bloomsbury Review:*

>—⊷•◯•⊶—<

The Bloomsbury Review: You've been published in major publications and you've won major prizes for your poetry. The best writers have said the best things about your poetry. But little of it is available to the public. Many of your books have gone out of print. I don't understand why more people don't know about your poetry outside of Colorado? Do you have any thoughts on this?

Thomas Hornsby Ferril: Frankly, I don't enjoy talking about poetry. I like to think that what I say in my poems is implicit and that each poem speaks for itself. I don't particularly enjoy doing interviews. I'd rather talk about plumbing or carpentry or any other kind of manual work. I enjoy things that you might not associate with poetry such as knife-throwing and tightrope-walking. I've enjoyed odd things like that during my life.

You work so hard on a poem to make it come out the way you want it to. I don't like to add anything to it in words. As far as availability of books goes, they come and go, they get printed and reprinted. Then they go out of print and sometimes they come back.

TBR: Is writing hard work for you?

THF: Yes. Any kind of writing is harder than working in a salt mine.

TBR: How did you get started in writing? Did you read a particular author or book that made you think, "I want to write." Who were your major influences?

THF: Well, I think it has to do with choosing the right parents. My mother was a very important influence on my life. She enjoyed poetry and we made rhymes together. My father, after I began writing, would bring home book after book of poetry. He thought that reading more poetry would help stimulate me to write, but it didn't work that way. I seldom opened the books. Later, of course, I did read many poets but never with the feeling that it would help my own writing.

I prefer technical journals and things like that. But I am happiest, I think, when I'm doing mechanical work. It keeps me away from this damn typewriter.

TBR: Do you ever give readings?

THF: I've never enjoyed getting together with groups and talking about poetry. People get into poetry groups and they talk it out instead of writing it out. Poetry is really a lonely business. I think you have to do it by yourself. Of course if you get into groups, that's another medium where you get to merchandise each other's reputations and I think that all distracts from poetry. The best poets I have known have been essentially lonely people.

TBR: What do you think about the way the West is being developed and exploited by the demand for fuel?

THF: Here in the West we are blundering into things we don't understand and won't understand until it begins to hurt. Then there's nothing we can do about it. These enormous skyscrapers they keep putting up! One of them requires as much water as a small town used to require, and the water simply isn't available. I think someday people will prowl through these skyscrapers as they prowl through Mesa Verde and say, "What sort of people did this? What in the world were they thinking about?" It's gotten out of hand. We're interested in the quick dollar and we don't worry about where the water is going to come from or what's going to happen to the Ogalala Aquifer or anything else. Then, when the thing becomes too difficult, we'll blunder in another direction.

TBR: There was a time in my life when I had the opportunity to be alone in the mountains for an extended period and I wanted to spend the time writing, but I found that the solitude drove me crazy. You've said that writing poetry is a very lonely business. How do you deal with the solitude?

THF: Well, I've done a lot of writing in the mountains, in my cabin. I've spent a lot of time up there in the summer and winter. It's the same opportunity or problem, whatever you want to call it, that you have right here, staring at the typewriter. I think it's illusory to think you can go to the mountains and seclude yourself. You have to fight it out with yourself whether you are in Denver, or Zanzibar, or Copenhagen, or wherever.

TBR: In conclusion, what is poetry?
THF: You might as well ask: What is life? What is love? I know many, many definitions of poetry. I guess they all add something. I think of poetry as a passionate apprehension of experience, ranging from agony to ecstasy, always stated concretely and overcast by feelings of transitoriness.

TRIBUTES TO THOMAS HORNSBY FERRIL

⊱—⊰⟩•○•⟨⊱—⊰

"A man is as tall as his height
Plus the height of his home town.
I know a Denverite
Who, measured from sea to crown,
Is one mile, five-foot ten,
And he swings a commensurate pen."

— **Robert Frost**

⊱—⊰⟩•○•⟨⊱—⊰

"He's terrifically and beautifully American. He is a poet, wit, historian, man of books and human affairs, and so definitely one of the Great Companions."

— **Carl Sandburg**

⊱—⊰⟩•○•⟨⊱—⊰

"It [Childe Herald] is by so far the best weekly column in contemporary journalism that there is no second place; the runner-up comes in third."

— **Bernard DeVoto,**
in *Harper's* magazine, on the *Herald's* most famous feature.

⊱—⊰⟩•○•⟨⊱—⊰

❈ 151 ❈

A Man to Match the Mountains

Duane A. Smith

>—⊶⟡⊷⟡⊶⟡⊶—<

Tom Ferril loved the mountains and mining fascinated him. Mountains and mining are the subjects of many of his poems, but he never let them over-power his writing. As he often stated, "Man and man alone is" the proper subject for the poet. When he combined the three, he produced some of his finest poetry—poetry that captures and captivates, that literally sings to the reader.

At his best, which he always was when writing about mountains and/or mining, Ferril moves the reader to feel and to sense. His active, strong, direct style captures the reader, carrying her or him along with Ferril. This is no more clearly shown than in the wonderfully moving, lyrical poem, "Magenta," in which he describes the life of a miner's wife in Central City. From its opening lines—"Once, up in Gilpin County, Colorado,/When a long blue afternoon was standing on end/Like a tombstone sinking into the Rocky Mountains, ..."—to the final period, the reader is transported back through the genera-tions. A sense of place, a sense of time for an era long gone emerges: the timelessness of the human spirit. The historian could not have done better. While he might not have called himself a historian, Ferril deserved the title, offering in his poetry a wonderful sense of people and time. "Magenta" ap-peared years before professional historians "discovered" women's history. Ferril might have exercised poetic license occasionally, but certainly that is in the realm of the poet!

His poem "Ghost Town" evokes the memory of "empty houses, hollow mountains," now that "the gold is gone." Never one to forsake the opportu-nity to give some advice, especially to the younger generation because he saw such "glorious dreams in the eyes of the children," Ferril concluded, "Dig in the earth for gold while you are young!"

More mystical is "Report of My Strange Encounter With Lily Bull-Domingo," in which he recounts an unusual "dream vision" he had in the Silver Cliff/Rosita country. The reader is left wondering about the past and the future, as well as the present mode of his encounter, which is probably exactly what Ferril intended. One of his longest poems about mountains and mining, "Words for Leadville," appears in a similar vein—"I walk alone up Harrison Avenue/Remembering ... remembering myself ... /But I remem-ber more than I remember ..." He envokes memories of gold and silver, of mines long abandoned, while challenging the reader to think, to ponder, to remember.

Of course, not all of Ferril's poems are about both mountains and mining. While he never let the overwhelming environment of the mountains dominate his poems, he understood them and their place in human existence. Few of his poems surpass "Time of Mountains" for its grace, simplicity, and emotion. The poem might be used as his epitaph:

So long ago my father led me to
The dark impounded orders of this canyon,
I have confused these rocks and water with
My life, but not unclearly, for I know
What will be here when I am here no more. ...

Birthday Boy

Gene Amole

>─┼─◆>─◯─<◆─┼─<

At some point Thursday, Thomas Hornsby Ferril will be introduced at a public gathering. He will be given a warm round of applause. After all, Tom is Colorado's poet laureate.

He will stand and smile modestly, and then he will make a gracious little speech telling how happy he is to be there. He will conclude by saying, "You have made this occasion very special for me, because today ... well, today is my birthday."

There will be one difference Thursday. I have it on the highest authority that February 25 is his real birthday anniversary. Tom has been known to give that little speech June 18, November 5, August 22, April 29, March 13, and on other dates only he can recall.

There is something inside Tom that makes him announce in public that it is his birthday, even when it isn't—*especially* when it isn't. He has never explained to me why he does this. I suspect it is because there is a lot of little boy in Tom Ferril. That's a good way to be when you turn 86, or 147, if you count all those other birthdays he has claimed.

There is no other American writer I admire more. Tom is incomparable. That is not just my view. Bernard de Voto described him as "the only first-rate poet in the West ... who happens to be one of the best writers of prose anywhere."

Carl Sandburg said of Tom: "He's terrifically and beautifully American.

And another Pulitzer Prize winner, Peter Viereck, wrote, "There is one very special emotion that Ferril conveys more movingly, more heart-breakingly than any other poet in American literature; the emotion of wist-fulness."

H.L. Mencken was a Ferril fan. He published some of his long poems, including "Magenta," in *The American Mercury*. In addition to his many books, Tom's work has also appeared in *The Atlantic, Harper's, The Saturday Review, Yale Review, The New Yorker, The New York Times,* and *Popular Mechanics*.

Popular Mechanics? Yes. The same man who wrote "Here Is a Land Where Life Is Written in Water," the text of the murals in the rotunda of the Colorado State Capitol, also sold an article to *Popular Mechanics* on how to bur-glar-proof cellar windows with old tire chains.

That's one of the many reasons Tom is so important to his many friends. He never lets his genius interfere with his humanity. I have never heard him talk down to anyone.

His poems are rich with the imagery of mountains, rivers, the plains, and the sky. In his "Time of Mountains," he wrote, "I have held rivers to my eyes like lenses,/And rearranged the mountains at my pleasure,/As one might change the apples in a bowl."

But his poetry is not about the natural environment. "Man is the subject of poetry, and man alone," Tom wrote. He loves mountains and rivers, but they are only his tools for implementing life. Ferril never forsakes the play for the setting.

For those who want to know him better, Channel 6 [has shown] "Tho-mas Hornsby Ferril, One Mile Five-Foot Ten." It is a 30-minute television portrait of Tom, a program produced by Don Kinney's Rocky Mountain Re-flections production company. It has been shown nationally on the Public Broadcasting System and has received an Emmy.

The program was a labor of love for those who worked on it, and it is their way of telling Tom how much they care for him.

(From the *Rocky Mountain News*, February 25, 1982.)

Ferril and Music

June M. Favre

The setting was the Denver Press Club, the time was early 1976, and Tom Ferril was the star holding court. The people sitting around the table were two or three generations younger than Ferril, but his topic of the day was C. W. McCall. We looked at one another, not having a clue as to who C. W. McCall was and why we should know who he was. Ferril proceeded to sing a few bars of "Convoy," a new song currently being played on some of the popular and country/western radio stations. The song, written by McCall, featured the language of Citizens' Band radio. After President Nixon signed into law the 55 mile-per-hour speed limit, Citizens' Band became a means for people to warn of speed traps on highways. Each CBer had his or her own "handle" or code name and would warn of the "Smokey" (patrol car) in the area. This appealed mightily to Ferril, who had picked up most of the CB lingo from the record, and also knew that C. W. McCall was an alias for William Fries.[1] Originally from Omaha, Fries was an advertising executive who, in the 1980s, was elected mayor of Ouray, Colorado.

This is an example of Ferril's wide-ranging interests, and those interests were abundantly apparent in the realm of music. From classical to country, Ferril was not limited to one type, style, or generation of music. His family home was filled with music and his writings make frequent reference to duets with Carl Sandburg — Sandburg on guitar, Ferril on mandolin. The mandolin became an obsession with Ferril. Before his teenage years, he decided he had to have a mandolin, but his mother told him there was no money to buy an instrument. He fell under the spell of the mandolin on a narrow gauge train ride one summer. "One summer morning along about 1906, maybe a year either way, we left Buena Vista, my parents, two sisters and I. Nearing the (Alpine) tunnel, the trainmen looked like bandits, their faces wrapped in wet bandannas. We were lost in a clatter of blackness and, incredible as it sounds, music! Delicate tinkling music! Two college boys were playing mandolins — a popular tune called 'Moonlight.' I was marked by 'Moonlight' forever." Ferril went on to recount his summer of yard work for "Miss Esther," and in September the hard-earned five silver dollars that bought him his first mandolin.[2]

As an entertainment writer for *The Denver Times*, Ferril had the assignment of interviewing Enrico Caruso, the Italian tenor. Undaunted by meeting one of the great celebrities of the day, Ferril confessed to the tenor that he had no experience as an interviewer. Caught off-guard by this unique approach, Caruso gave a relaxed and candid interview to the novice reporter.[3] In his position at *The Denver Times*, Ferril had the opportunity to meet and write about a wide variety of music and musical performers. His March 1921 column, titled *Jazz Scales Parnassus*, defends the jazz idiom, which faced formidable foes in America but found a home in Europe. "The learned American musician, when queried on it, tip-tilts his nose like the petal of the flower and condescends that possibly its tempo is interesting, but little more." The column closed with the comment, "Who knows but, one of these days, in one of our esoteric recitals in the auditorium, some touted Jascha or Mischa or Sacha will be playing absolute jazz ... variations on a theme from 'I'll Say She Does,' or Irving Berlin's fugue in C minor, opus 27, after Brahms!"[4]

Perhaps the culmination of Ferril's musical aspirations came in 1956 when Cecil Effinger's *Fourth Symphony for Chorus and Orchestra* was televised by NBC for *Wide Wide World* with Ferril reading from *Words for Time*. The collaboration would continue with Effinger's *Four Pastorales* based on four of Ferril's short poems and in 1979 with *Suite for Two Flutes and Voices* also featuring four poems: "By Seven Senses," "Swallows," "Odd Day in Springtime," and "I Sawed a Log." [5]

A genuine love of music in all forms was evident throughout Ferril's entire life, from childhood memories, singing lessons given by Wilberforce Whiteman, playing in bands to raise money for college tuition, concerts and operas, and surely part of his attraction to Helen Ray. Hellie and Tom were married in 1921. A statuesque beauty, Hellie had contemplated a singing career, but settled instead for nursing before turning to editing *The Rocky Mountain Herald*. Friends remember her lovely, clear voice, which in later years was exhibited at birthday parties with a wrenching delivery of *My Sweetheart Went Down on the "Maine."*

Tom Ferril and music cannot be separated. His life was devoted to melody, lyric, and meter. He once remarked that he was making a list of all the songs he knew and the list contained more than 2,000 titles. We aren't talking about knowing just the melodies of these songs, but knowing verse and chorus or choruses! On his walks around City Park Lake, now renamed "Ferril Lake," he would be whistling or humming a continuous stream of melodies. He was never without music in his heart, in his soul, and in his writing.

---

1. *Lissauer's Encyclopedia of Popular Music in America/The Comprehensive Country Music Encyclopedia*
2. *Rocky Mountain News*, Sunday, August 27, 1978
3. *The Denver Times*, October 20, 1920
4. *The Denver Times*, March 26, 1921
5. *Rocky Mountain News*, Friday, January 19, 1979

Ferril and Nature

Tom Cooper

>─┤◆>─○─<◆┤─<

"Now, Cooper, if we just shinny up that log ahead, we can make it over the big rock to the top."

Tom Ferril, well over sixty, climbed the thirty-foot long sloping pine and the two of us were there, looking down on the falls of remote Craig Creek in the central Colorado Rockies.

"Over there," he pointed toward the upper valley, "were herds of elk. The Indians came up here to hunt them. And buffalo! The last wild herd survived between here and Lost Park!"

Tom loved this wild country. He had roamed the mountains since he was a boy. The beauty of his poetry stems from an intimate, loving knowledge of the creeks he fished, the trails he walked, and the old mining towns he explored.

But back to the falls. We both scanned the sparkling pool at the base for rising trout. Instead, what we saw was a group of small, sleek animals diving and playing in the bubbling pool. Beaver? Neither of us had seen such playful ones. Ferril yelled, "Otter! That's what those are, freshwater otter! Nobody has spotted them up here for years!"

We watched as the little otter, most playful of animals, frolicked in their mountain hideaway. Half an hour passed, then we climbed back down the mountain and out of the valley.

Some days later, Tom's friend, Bob Niedrach, curator of the Denver Museum of Natural History, verified our rare sighting of the almost extinct Rocky Mountain otter, an animal not spotted since 1906.

The Poet as
Landmark Commissioner

Edward D. White, Jr.

Four years before his appointment to the Denver Landmark Preservation Commission, Thomas Hornsby Ferril, in his November 22, 1969, "Childe Herald" column, addressed the "mindless" destruction of historic buildings in downtown Denver. "My inclination to write with anger," he conceded, "is overcome by feelings of sadness and pity for the kind of thinking that goes on in Denver: ... the past is meaningless; automobiles are more important than people; the Sacred Bulldozer is supreme!"

As Colorado's revered indigenous poet, Ferril brought fresh insights and historic perspectives to the fledging Landmark Commission's mixed membership of architects, historians, matrons, and civic benefactors. It was a critical period in the evolution of public responsibility for future preservation of the historic urban environment. To Ferril, however, Denver's history was the living past, recorded in layers of remembered time back to the pristine prairie. Of the landmark Daniels & Fisher Tower he wrote:

> Off to the west downtown
> is a tower with a clock that keeps
> some sort of time
> that seems to be in fashion
> now and then.
>
> It doesn't bother me
> for well I knew that space of air
> long before the tower was there,
> back when the earth
> this flagstone covers
> was in flower
> with prairie primroses ...

During a 1973 public hearing on the landmark qualifications of the Herman Heisser House, a Victorian monument noted for its Queen Ann tower and elegant side porch overlooking an expansive yard, Ferril recalled, to an astonished audience, that William Jennings Bryan had delivered a campaign speech from that very porch in the summer of 1908, during the Democratic national convention in Denver's new City Auditorium. At twelve years of age, Tom had already become the omnipresent observer and great rememberer of old Denver; his distinctive contribution to Landmark Commission deliberations 65 years later was his unflagging recollection of forgotten Denver lore. Enthusiasts in the audience, eager for knowledge about Denver's historic people and places, would ask Tom where in local libraries and archives they could find his sources of information. "You can't," Tom would retort. "You have to ask me."

Soon after Ferril's appointment in 1973, the Commission undertook the designation of the Ferril House at 2123 Downing Street. It was understood that Ferril was himself the landmark, and the family house marked the historic site of his life and achievement. Still unschooled in landmark protocol, the city decided to delay the plaque installation until the following spring. Helen Ferril was in failing health, however, and her anxiety over the plaque delay led to an appeal from Tom for action. Addressed to Commission Chairman Ed White and dated "November 13, 1973 A.D.," his letter began: "For personal reasons you would sympathize with, were I to go into them, I'd like to see the plaque go up soon and not wait for spring." "I can put it up myself," he offered. "I'm a genius with Epoxy and other kindred goop. If the pressed brick is chilly, on our front porch wall, I can warm it up. I have torches, electric heaters, and secret devices known only to the Atomic Energy Commission." The plaque was cast, engraved, and installed before Thanksgiving.

Tom Ferril resigned as Landmark Commissioner at the end of his first three-year term on his eightieth birthday, February 25, 1976, the Colorado Centennial year. He had been a participant and rememberer of life in Denver since 1896. He was indeed the *stuff* of Colorado history—a primary source, rather than a latter-day preservationist. Today's historic landmarks were Ferril's living memories, "that years can touch only if years remember how flame can burn too clean to leave an ember."

We Try to Celebrate

Jack Kisling

>━┼━◆>━┼━O━┼━<◆━┼━<

In 1976, which was Thomas Hornsby Ferril's 80th year, he gave us a poem
entitled "Stories of Three Summers" to help us plumb our Centennial-Bicen-
tennial feelings. In it he took us into three summers scattered over three
centuries, declaring:

> I who tell those stories of three summers
> Must not let allegory blunt
> My plain intention
> To interweave old tales of Colorado
> With deeds of far-off patriots long ago
> We try to celebrate
> By mere coincidence
> Of dates on calendars
>
> Like saying *Happy Birthday*
> To ourselves
> As we click a stop-watch on oblivion.

By habit and example, Thomas Hornsby Ferril has spent a lifetime help-
ing us as we try to celebrate. Now, as we undertake to celebrate him, it is
heartening to think that little by little we grasp the idea he's been showing us
all along, which is how to celebrate ourselves.

When we first began to get the hang of this we painted his words in a
gilded ring around our state capitol's rotunda and stood back looking at them
with pride and wonder. Others of his words we cast in bronze and bolted to
a wall where two of our puny streams meet and seem somehow less puny for
those words' being there.

We have brought our account up to date by officially proclaiming Tom
Ferril the laureate he has in truth been for many decades.

We have affixed a bronze medallion to his home on Downing Street. It
helps us measure the marvel of this man who simply won't industrialize, in-
sisting instead on remaining a cottage industry. We look at the plaque and
say: "Right here is where Tom Ferril grew up and reared his family and lives
and writes those poems. And we *know* him. Why, he might be upstairs there
writing one right now."

And he might be. Up there privately probing the unprofitable, turning
the little and forgotten and hazy into the large and memorable and exact.

We've never known quite how to pay this poet for such treasure, as his daughter Anne understood years ago when she told an inquiring school teacher that "Father is a poet but he works for the sugar company that we may eat."

But we try to celebrate. We notice him, here with a plaque, there with a medal, now and then with an honorary degree. And even though in the very length of his life he has shown us that our least concern should be with boundaries, we continue to debate his boundaries. Is he a regional poet, or national, or worldwide, or what? Is he one of our stray lambs, transformed by time into one of our shepherds? Should we erect a statue to him, and if so, would it be appropriate for Tom Ferril to be carved in granite wearing that thick old tweed sport coat with the leather piping around the collar and cuffs? Would it compromise posterity to have him grasping a mandolin? Wearing his most quizzical smile?

Knowing so little of such matters, should we presume to try saying something timeless about him?

Perhaps it's best to have him do the timeless talking for us, as he did in the closing stanzas of "Stories of Three Summers."

Do I hear terror singing into laughter?
Do I hear torture gasping into love?
Dare I believe more dreams than I can prove?
We never never know until long after

If even then

(Written for the occasion celebrating Thomas Hornsby Ferril's work at the Western History Department of the Denver Public Library.)

Ferril's Vision
of the American West

Bill Hornby

>─┤─◆〉─○─〈◆─├─<

If you're new to Thomas Hornsby Ferril, in this anthology you've unexpect-
edly struck one of the richer veins in Rocky Mountain and Colorado culture.
Ferril's work, herein amply sampled, has been slipping out of print, just as
he's been slipping out of the memory of all but his fiercely loyal old gang.
They're much indebted to Bob Baron of Fulcrum Publishing and to the Uni-
versity of Colorado's Center of the American West for lighting Tom's one-
hundredth birthday with this candle of recollection.

It is no surprise that Ferril's work is a surprise. Since he began, Colorado
and the West's population have multiplied, now millions instead of thousands.
Our region is still a newcomer's land, and as anywhere in a highly mobile
society, the bulk of them pack in their culture instead of digging it out of their
new place.

But doggedly, over less than two centuries of urban existence, our Western
American publishers, historians, writers, musicians, painters, poets, archi-
tects, artists, and other creators have been forming a solid regional culture. It
has slowly penetrated attention back "in the states" and across the seas, and
Ferril has been part of that penetration, although not as big a part as he
should be.

In 1987 the Western Literature Association published the mammoth *Lit-
erary History of the American West* (Texas Christian University Press, Fort
Worth), some 1,400 pages of literature that demolishes the concept that the
West has no regional culture worth notice. Of the Rocky Mountain writers
cut out of the herd for individual chapters in this landmark work, we find
Vardis Fisher, Bernard DeVoto, A. B. Guthrie Jr., Frank Waters, Jack
Schaefer, Wallace Stegner, Walter Van Tilburg Clark — and Thomas Hornsby
Ferril! Not a bad bunch to ride with.

But do these "regional" writers have much to say around the campfires
of the global village? Will they be as helpful in the West of the twenty-first
century as in our waning twentieth? Does following Tom Ferril into the next
century give any sign of a clear trail? Would anyone sign on to the World
Wide Web "home page" at http://www.ferril.com?

There are, in my ardent fan's belief, some Ferril visions that will be even
more useful to Westerners in the future than they have been in the past.

In his poems, Ferril's West is a whole West. The mountains erode into the plains, as do the distinctions between them. People rise from and return to the earth of the place, and they are an integral part of nature, not its invasive opponents.

Another Ferril theme—there always has been and always will be as much, if not more, of failure in the West as of success. The subject in the poem "Magenta," the abandoned dress-maker's dummy, is a Western symbol as much as the triumphal explorer. The miners come up from a morning below to bury their burnt-out women in the afternoon.

Cities are as much the stuff of the West as the great outdoors. Ferril lived his thoroughly Western life in one town and one house, and loved the Denver streets through which he could make out the far-blue Rockies, his other home. Neighboring was as Western to him as being alone in the mountains. He knew both why the wreath was hanging on the next-door porch and where to find his fishing hole. There was no urban-rural split in his philosophy.

Science and technology are admissible in Ferril's vision of the real West. He was as fascinated by the parts of a bluegrass stem or of a flower poking up through the cracks of a ghost home as by the old engine on the junk heap. Ferril balanced science and nature, including nature's people. Such philosophical balance might restore our West in coming years.

And above all, Ferril's West is very much part of the broader world, not an escape hatch from it. He relates his West to Greece and Rome, not to dress-up cowboys. Nor is he centered on any one ethnic or gender version of history. In his West, the Spanish come in first, and the Indians are here to receive them. His is not the "empty" West of some manifestly destined, nationalistic definition.

For the escapist and loner in the West, Ferril is no soother. To him, "landscape is simply a static stage; it requires the movements of people, clouds, storms, the coming and going of vegetation, and most of all, human experience applied to these movements … ." This is from the early essay "Rocky Mountain Metaphysics," which warns creators not to be dominated by awe of the mountains or nature. A mountain is a "great wall behind which something is forever happening."

Welcome to Thomas Hornsby Ferril's vision of the American West. It will serve us well in the new century if we dig it out and reabsorb it.

List of Contributors

GENE AMOLE is an author and a radio broadcaster, and a longtime columnist with the *Rocky Mountain News*.

TOM AUER is the publisher of *The Bloomsbury Review*. He feels honored that he had the opportunity to talk to Mr. Ferril, even though he was not willing to talk much about his poetry.

ROBERT C. BARON is a publisher and writer. His books include *The Garden and Farm Books of Thomas Jefferson, Soul of America*, and *20th Century America — Key Events in History*.

DR. JOHN C. BUECHNER is President of the University of Colorado.

TOM COOPER, a longtime Denver businessman and friend of the Ferril family, knew Mr. Ferril for more than 40 years; they shared a deep interest in mountains and in the arts.

BERNARD DEVOTO (1892–1955) was an American historian, novelist, critic, and editor of *Harper's* magazine. He won the Pulitzer Prize for History in 1948 for his book *Across the Wide Missouri*.

JUNE M. FAVRE is a performer, dramatist, and writer, and has received the Denver Mayor's Award for Excellence in the Arts. She has brought Ferril's work to the stage and television.

ANNE FERRIL FOLSOM, Thomas Hornsby Ferril's daughter, is a writer and illustrator. Her books include *The American Bestiary, The Care and Training of Husbands, The Indoor Bird Watcher's Manual*, and *I Hate Thursday*.

ROBERT FROST (1874–1963) was an American poet who chiefly wrote about New England. He won numerous honors and awards, including four Pulitzer Prizes for American Poetry.

BILL HORNBY is the former editor of *The Denver Post* and a longtime trustee of the Colorado Historical Society.

JACK KISLING, a lifelong journalist, is a columnist with *The Denver Post.*, where he has practiced his art since 1968 and describes himself as a protegé of Ferril's at the Denver Press Club.

STEPHEN J. LEONARD is a Western historian. His books include *Denver: From Mining Camp to Metropolis, Colorado: A History of the Centennial State*, and *Trials and Triumphs*.

PATRICIA NELSON LIMERICK is a history educator. Her books include *Legacy of Conquest, Desert Passages, Trails: Towards a New Western History*, and *The Frontier in American Culture*.

THOMAS J. NOEL is a Western historian. His books include *Denver: From Mining Camp to Metropolis, Colorado: The Highest State*, and *Historical Atlas of Colorado*.

CARL SANDBURG (1878–1967) was a poet, folklorist, historian, and children's author. He won the Pulitzer Prize in History for *Abraham Lincoln — the War Years* (1940) and in poetry for *Complete Poems* (1951).

DUANE A. SMITH is a history educator. His books include *Rocky Mountain Mining Camps, Rocky Mountain West, Horace Tabor*, and *Mining America*.

EDWARD D. WHITE, JR., restoration architect and architectural historian, has served on the Denver Landmark Preservation Commission since 1969.

Bibliography

>--+--•--+--<

The majority of Thomas Hornsby Ferril's poetry was first published in newspapers and magazines. He published his first poem at the age of nine in 1905. Much of his prose was published in *The Rocky Mountain Herald* between 1939 and 1972. Ferril was an editorial writer, drama, film, and book reviewer for the *Denver Times* from June 25, 1919, to August 6, 1921, and served as a drama and film critic for the *Rocky Mountain News* from November 5, 1922, to December 27, 1925.

Ferril's poems and essays have appeared in *American Heritage, The American Mercury, American Poetry Magazine, Atlantic Monthly, Colorado Quarterly, Denver Times, Harper's, New Republic, The Nation, The New Yorker, New York Herald Tribune Books, The New York Times Magazine, Rocky Mountain News, Saturday Review of Literature, Scribner's Magazine, The Yale Review,* and elsewhere.

A complete list of Ferril's publications through 1960 is contained in Robert Fulton Richards' Ph.D. dissertation, "The Poetry of Thomas Hornsby Ferril" (New York: Columbia University English Department, 1961), which is available from University Microfilms in Ann Arbor, Michigan. See also the Thomas Hornsby Ferril manuscript collection in the Western History Department of the Denver Public Library.

Poetry by Ferril

Anvil of Roses. Boise, Idaho: Ahsahta Press, Boise State University, 1983. 50 p.

High Passage. New Haven: Yale University Press, 1926. Reprinted New York: AMS Press, 1971. 50 p.

New & Selected Poems. New York: Harper and Brothers, 1952. Reprinted Westport, Conn.: Greenwood Press, 1970. 182 p.

Trial by Time. New York: Harper and Brothers, 1944. 120 p.

Westering. New Haven: Yale University Press, 1934. Reprinted Boise, Idaho: Ahsahta Press, Boise State University, 1986. 82 p.

Words for Denver and Other Poems. New York: William Morrow, 1966. 96 p.

Prose by Ferril

I Hate Thursday. New York: Harper & Brothers, 1946. 240 p.

Letters of the Pike's Peak Gold Rush, by Libeus Barney, introduction by Thomas Hornsby Ferril. San Jose, Calif.: Talisman Press, 1959. 98 p.

The Rocky Mountain Herald Reader. New York: William Morrow, 1966. 302 p.

White Churches of the Plains, by Robert H. Adams, foreword by Thomas Hornsby Ferril. Boulder, Colo.: Colorado Associated University Press, 1970. 84 p.

Works on Ferril

Richards, Robert F. "Literature and Politics." *Colorado Quarterly,* 19 (summer 1970), 97–106.

———. "Science, Ferril, and Poetry." *Prairie Schooner,* 21 (fall 1947), 312–18.

———. "The Long Dimension of Ferril's Poetry." *Colorado Quarterly,* 3 (summer 1954), 22–38.

———. "Thomas Hornsby Ferril and the Problems of the Poet in the West." *Kansas Quarterly,* 2 (spring 1970), 110–16.

Roe, Margie McCreless. "Thomas Hornsby Ferril, Poet and Critic of the Rocky Mountain Region." Master's thesis, Southern Methodist University, 1966.

Scherting, Jack. "An Approach to the Western Poetry of Thomas Hornsby Ferril." *Western American Literature,* 7 (fall 1972), 179–90.

Trusky, A. Thomas. *Thomas Hornsby Ferril.* Boise, Idaho: Boise State College, 1973. 52 p.

Musical Collaborations (with Cecil Effinger)

Four Pastorales for Oboe and Chorus (from Ferril's "No Mark," "Noon," "Basket," and "Wood"). New York: G. Schirmer, 1962.

Let Your Mind Wander Over America (from Ferril's "Let Your Mind Wander Over America"). New York: G. Schirmer, 1969.

Set of Three for Chorus and Brass (from Ferril's "This Trail," "Trial by Time," and "Inner Song While Watching a Square Dance"). Bryn Mawr, Penn.: Elkan-Vogel [Presser], 1961.

Symphony for Chorus and Orchestra (from Ferril's "Words for Time"). New York: Carl Fischer, 1952.

Recording by Ferril

"Thomas Hornsby Ferril Reading His Own Poems." Library of Congress, Division of Music, Order No. LWO 1734 (December 1, 1950).